EDUCATION IN AFRICA

MASON CREST
PHILADELPHIA

EDUCATION IN AFRICA

Suzanne Grant Lewis

MC **Mason Crest**
PHILADELPHIA

Frontispiece: nda.

Mason Crest
450 Parkway Drive, Suite D
Broomall, PA 19008
www.masoncrest.com

Printed and bound in the United States of America.

CPSIA Compliance Information: Batch #APP2013. For further information, contact Mason Crest at 1-866-MCP-Book

First printing
1 3 5 7 9 8 6 4 2

Library of Congress Cataloging-in-Publication Data

Lewis, Suzanne Grant.
  Education in Africa / Suzanne Grant Lewis.
      p. cm. — (Africa: progress and problems)
  Includes bibliographical references and index.
  ISBN 978-1-4222-2938-5 (hc)
  ISBN 978-1-4222-8883-2 (ebook)
  1. Education—Africa. I. Title.
  LA1501.L48 2013
  370.96—dc23
                            2013013026

Africa: Progress and Problems series ISBN: 978-1-4222-2934-7

Table of Contents

AFRICA: PROGRESS AND PROBLEMS

THE PROMISE OF TODAY'S AFRICA

by Robert I. Rotberg

Today's Africa is a mosaic of effective democracy and desperate despotism, immense wealth and abysmal poverty, conscious modernity and mired traditionalism, bitter conflict and vast arenas of peace, and enormous promise and abiding failure. Generalizations are more difficult to apply to Africa or Africans than elsewhere. The continent, especially the sub-Saharan two-thirds of its immense landmass, presents enormous physical, political, and human variety. From snow-capped peaks to intricate patches of remaining jungle, from desolate deserts to the greatest rivers, and from the highest coastal sand dunes anywhere to teeming urban conglomerations, Africa must be appreciated from myriad perspectives. Likewise, its peoples come in every shape and size, govern themselves in several complicated manners, worship a host of indigenous and imported gods, and speak thousands of original and five or six derivative common languages. To know Africa is to know nuance and complexity.

There are 54 nation-states that belong to the African Union, 49 of which are situated within the sub-Saharan mainland or on its offshore islands. No other continent has so many countries, political divisions, or members of the General Assembly of the United Nations. No other continent encompasses so many distinctively different peoples or spans such geographical disparity. On no other continent have so many innocent civilians lost their lives in intractable civil wars—15 million since 1991 in such places as Algeria, Angola, the Congo, Côte d'Ivoire, Liberia, Sierra Leone, and Sudan. No other continent has so many disparate natural resources (from cadmium, cobalt, and copper to petroleum and zinc) and so little to show for their frenzied exploitation. No other continent has proportionally so many people subsisting (or trying to) on less than $2 a day. But then no other continent has been so beset by HIV/AIDS (30 percent of all adults in southern Africa), by tuberculosis, by malaria (prevalent almost everywhere), and by less well-known scourges such as schistosomiasis (liver fluke), several kinds of filariasis, river blindness, trachoma, and trypanosomiasis (sleeping sickness).

Africa is among the most Christian continents, but it also is home to more Muslims than the Middle East. Apostolic and Pentecostal churches are immensely powerful. So are Sufi brotherhoods. Yet traditional African religions are still influential. So is a belief in spirits and witches (even among Christians and Muslims), in faith healing and in alternative medicine. Polygamy remains popular. So does the practice of female circumcision and other long-standing cultural preferences. Africa cannot be well understood without appreciating how village life still permeates the great cities and how urban pursuits engulf villages. Africa can no longer be considered predominantly rural, agricultural, or wild; more than half of its peoples live in towns and cities.

Political leaders must cater to both worlds, old and new. They and their followers must join the globalized, Internet-

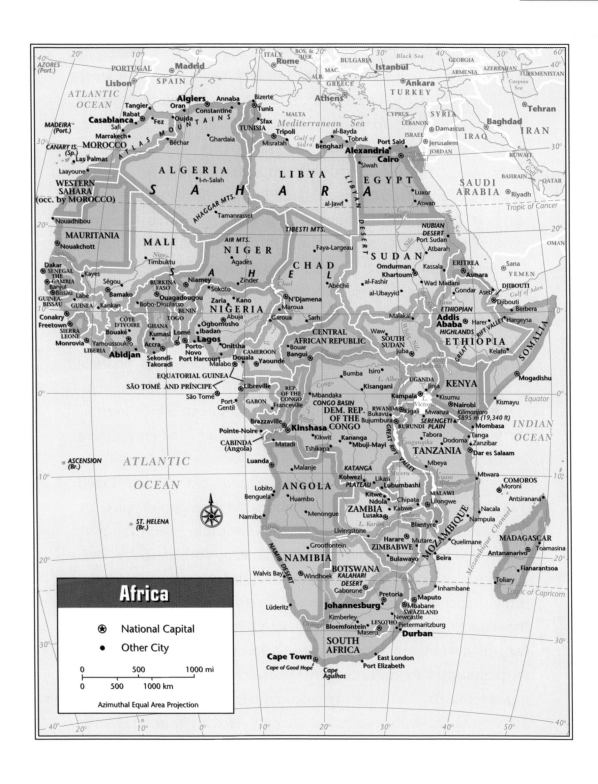

Africa

⊛ National Capital

• Other City

0   500   1000 mi

0   500   1000 km

Azimuthal Equal Area Projection

penetrated world even as they remain rooted appropriately in past modes of behavior, obedient to dictates of family, lineage, tribe, and ethnicity. This duality often results in democracy or at least partially participatory democracy. Equally often it develops into autocracy. Botswana and Mauritius have enduring democratic governments. In Benin, Ghana, Kenya, Lesotho, Malawi, Mali, Mozambique, Namibia, Nigeria, Senegal, South Africa, Tanzania, and Zambia fully democratic pursuits are relatively recent and not yet sustainably implanted. Algeria, Cameroon, Chad, the Central African Republic, Egypt, the Sudan, and Tunisia are authoritarian entities run by strongmen. Zimbabweans and Equatorial Guineans suffer from even more venal rule. Swazis and Moroccans are subject to the real whims of monarchs. Within even this vast sweep of political practice there are still more distinctions. The partial democracies represent a spectrum. So does the manner in which authority is wielded by kings, by generals, and by long-entrenched civilian autocrats.

The democratic countries are by and large better developed and more rapidly growing economically than those ruled by strongmen. In Africa there is an association between the pursuit of good governance and beneficial economic performance. Likewise, the natural resource wealth curse that has afflicted mineral-rich countries such as the Congo and Nigeria has had the opposite effect in well-governed places like Botswana. Nation-states open to global trade have done better than those with closed economies. So have those countries with prudent managements, sensible fiscal arrangements, and modest deficits. Overall, however, the bulk of African countries have suffered in terms of reduced economic growth from the sheer fact of being tropical, beset by disease in an enervating climate where there is an average of one trained physician to every 13,000 persons. Many lose growth prospects, too, because of the absence of navigable rivers, the paucity of ocean and river ports, barely maintained roads, and few and narrow railroads. Moreover, 15 of Africa's countries are landlocked, without comfortable access to relatively inexpensive waterborne transport. Hence, imports and exports for much of Africa are more expensive than elsewhere as they move over formidable distances. Africa is the most underdeveloped continent because of geographical and health constraints that have not yet been overcome, because of ill-considered policies, because of the sheer number of separate nation-states (a colonial legacy), and because of poor governance.

Africa's promise is immense, and far more exciting than its achievements have been since a wave of nationalism and independence in the 1960s liberated nearly every section of the continent. Thus, the next several decades of the 21st century are ones of promise for Africa. The challenges are clear: to alleviate grinding poverty and deliver greater real economic goods to larger proportions of people in each country, and across all countries; to deliver more of the benefits of good governance to more of Africa's peoples; to end the destructive killing fields that run rampant across so much of Africa; to improve educational training and health services; and to roll back the scourges of HIV/AIDS, tuberculosis, and malaria. Every challenge represents an opportunity with concerted and bountiful Western assistance to transform the lives of Africa's vulnerable and resourceful future generations.

1 OVERVIEW: THE PROMISE OF EDUCATION IN AFRICA

This young student in Rwanda is learning to read and write with the aid of a chalkboard. Education, the key to unlocking the potential of individuals, can also play a crucial role in improving political, social, and economic conditions throughout sub-Saharan Africa.

bservers inside and outside Africa characterize education on the continent as being in a state of crisis. By many indications, this is accurate. There are over 40 million children in Africa who are not in school. Schools are ill equipped, suffering shortages of most types of supplies, from chalk and textbooks to library books and lab chemicals. A large number of schools, especially at lower primary grades, hold classes outside under trees. A significant percentage of schools have no water or electricity, let alone a telephone, photocopier, or computer.

At the same time, tremendous progress has been made in eliminating the discriminatory practices that were the norm as recently as 40 years ago, which kept African children out of school. Across the continent, education systems have experimented with more relevant curricula, revamped examination systems, forged regional research networks, and instituted democratic school governance models.

Education serves as a social control, reproducing society and reflecting all its inequalities. But education also offers a critique of society and can change or even revolutionize it. Education has the power to liberate individuals; literacy can open the world and help people reach their potential. For a society emerging from an oppressive system of government, education can be crucial in the definition and pursuit of a new vision. Education can be the promise of lasting peace. It is seen as the means to improve a country's standard of living because it develops "human capital." Education is a prerequisite for engagement on the global stage.

NO PANACEA

Some people believe that education can provide the cure for every social ill, be it unemployment, poor economic conditions, or social unrest. This is a misconception, albeit one that is widely held in many parts of the world, including Africa.

Students at the Karimba School in northern Kenya.

Very often when we speak of education we really mean schooling, even though education is much more than that. Education takes place in many settings other than a classroom. It occurs through formal and informal processes, on the job, at cultural events, through the media, and at community gatherings.

The education statistics from Africa are often conflicting and incomplete. At times statistics refer to the whole continent, including North Africa, while at other times the data includes only sub-Saharan African countries. Generally, there are fewer educational opportunities in sub-Saharan Africa than in the northern part of the continent, and this is reflected in lower enrollment figures when data from just sub-Saharan Africa is used. In addition to this limitation, local data is difficult to find, and there is usually significant variation in educational experiences across regions of a single country. It should be kept in mind that while the statistics provide windows for understanding educational conditions in Africa, they do not capture the full reality. It is important also to learn about the numerous initiatives in Africa that aim to fulfill the many promises of education on the continent.

EDUCATIONAL PARTICIPATION IN AFRICA AND THE WORLD

In 2000, 189 member states of the United Nations (UN) committed themselves to a set of eight Millennium Development Goals (MDGs). The MDGs aim to reduce extreme poverty in its many forms by 2015. Since education is seen as a way out of poverty for individuals and societies, two of the goals pertain to education. Goal 2 is to achieve universal primary education. The target is to ensure that all children, regardless of gender or circumstance, can complete primary school. Goal 3 is to promote gender equality and empower women. The focus is on ensuring gender parity—that is, that an equal proportion of females and males are enrolled in each level of education.

In addition to the MDGs, various countries have pledged to support education through the Education for All (EFA) initiative, launched in 1990 at the World Conference on Education for All in Jomtein, Thailand. The follow-up EFA Conference in Dakar, Senegal, in 2000 conceded that most countries had fallen far short of the

EFA goals, and 164 governments recommitted themselves by signing the Dakar Framework for Action. While the MDGs cover a wide range of development issues, including education, the more detailed and ambitious EFA goals are focused solely on education.

Responsibility for monitoring progress toward the achievement of the MDGs and the EFA goals falls to governments as well as international bodies, including various arms of the United Nations Development Programme, UNESCO (the United

DAKAR EDUCATION FOR ALL FRAMEWORK FOR ACTION

(i) expanding and improving comprehensive early childhood care and education, especially for the most vulnerable and disadvantaged children;

(ii) ensuring that by 2015 all children, particularly girls, children in difficult circumstances, and those belonging to ethnic minorities, have access to and complete free and compulsory primary education of good quality;

(iii) ensuring that the learning needs of all young people and adults are met through equitable access to appropriate learning and life skills programs;

(iv) achieving a 50 percent improvement in levels of adult literacy by 2015, especially for women, and equitable access to basic and continuing education for all adults;

(v) eliminating gender disparities in primary and secondary education by 2005, and achieving gender equality in education by 2015, with a focus on ensuring girls' full and equal access to and achievement in basic education of good quality;

(vi) improving all aspects of the quality of education and ensuring excellence of all so that recognized and measurable learning outcomes are achieved by all, especially in literacy, numeracy, and essential life skills.

Nations Educational, Scientific and Cultural Organization), UNICEF (the United Nations Children's Fund), and the UN Millennium Project, an independent advisory body to the UN. The reports issued by these organizations provide data and analysis on Africa's educational situation and offer a basis for comparison with other regions of the world.

PREPRIMARY EDUCATION

Access to preprimary education is very limited in sub-Saharan Africa. Preprimary schooling is most available in urban areas, and because of the costs it is often only accessible to wealthier households. "On average, a child in Africa can expect only 0.3 years of pre-primary schooling," states the 2005 EFA Global Monitoring Report, "compared to 1.6 years in Latin America and the Caribbean and 2.2 years in North America and Western Europe."

In Uganda, as in most developing countries, more boys attend school than girls. Often, girls are needed at home to gather water and help run the household.

TABLE 2
SECONDARY NET ENROLLMENT RATIOS BY REGION[a]

REGION	ENROLLMENT RATIO			GENDER GAP
	TOTAL	MALE	FEMALE	
Africa[c]	26	29	23	−4
Asia[c]	88	89	87	−2
Oceania	70	69	71	+2
Europe	81	82	80	−2
North America	90	90	91	+1
South America[b]	73	71	76	+5

a.   Net enrollment ratios count only pupils of the official school age, and therefore figures cannot be greater than 100%.
b.   Includes Central America and the Caribbean.
c.   UIS estimate for gender figures.
Source: UIS Global Education Digest 2010, p. 147.

TABLE 3
GROSS ENROLLMENT RATIOS IN POSTSECONDARY EDUCATION BY REGION

REGION	GROSS ENROLLMENT RATIO
Sub-Saharan Africa	6
World total	26
North America & Western Europe	70
Central & Eastern Europe	64
Central Asia	25
Arab States	21
Latin America & Caribbean	38
East Asia/Oceania	26
South & West Asia	13

Source: UIS Global Education Digest 2010, p. 170.

FIGURE 1
DISTRIBUTION OF OUT-OF-SCHOOL YOUTH BY REGION

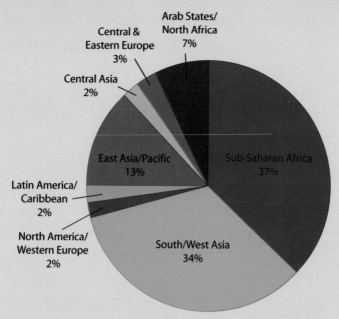

Source: UNESCO *EFA Global Monitoring Report.*

FIGURE 2
DISTRIBUTION OF ADULT ILLITERATES BY REGION

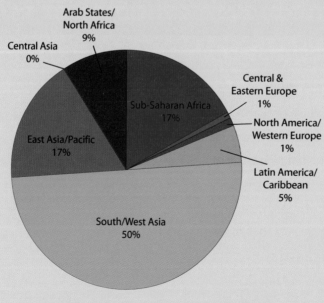

Source: UNESCO *EFA Global Monitoring Report.*

these out-of-school children—37 percent of the world total—are in sub-Saharan Africa, despite efforts in the region to increase enrollment. Of sub-Saharan Africa's 40.3 million children of primary school age who do not attend school, approximately 55 percent are girls.

Regional data concerning out-of-school children provides the big picture, but to better understand who these children are and how they might be reached, it is necessary to break down the population by gender, wealth, geography, and ethnicity. These categories are interrelated. Among the richest families, there tends to be no difference between boys' and girls' participation in education. But among poor families, there is a greater chance that girls will not attend school or will not attend for as many years as boys. Poor girls in rural Africa are the most likely not to attend school.

ADULT LITERACY EDUCATION

The background documents from the World Conference on Education for All note that the map of the underdeveloped world (measured by poverty and access to basic necessities) and the map of world illiteracy correspond. Literacy, most development specialists believe, opens doors to opportunity. Sub-Saharan Africa is home to about 20 percent of the approximately 1 billion adults (defined as age 15 or older) in the world who are illiterate. About 61 percent of these people are female. To break the numbers down a different way, in sub-Saharan Africa about 70 percent of the adult males are literate, but only 50 percent of the adult females can read and write.

HISTORICAL ROOTS OF CONTEMPORARY EDUCATION

The Western school model is ubiquitous throughout the world. A visitor to a school in, for example, rural Guinea would recognize it as a school. It would likely have a line of classrooms, and inside each the visitor would see blackboards, a teacher's desk, and rows of desks and benches. It might be constructed from different building materials, but it would be recognizable as a school.

Despite a common physical appearance, the educational system of every society is different in important ways, having developed through unique historical conditions incorporating specific social, economic, political, and cultural influences. Educational systems throughout contemporary Africa are the product of three major forces: indigenous education; religion, primarily Christianity and Islam; and colonialism.

INDIGENOUS EDUCATION

In most cases, the primary purpose of education is to ensure the continuation of the society, sustaining its development and providing a means for social control. It should be remembered that education is not synonymous with formal schooling. In Africa indigenous education, also called traditional education, existed for centuries before the introduction of formal schooling. Although many features of this kind of education have been lost over the centuries, some features survive.

Historically, indigenous education served to socialize youth in the ways of the community and develop abilities, beliefs, and behaviors that would allow them to become contributing members of society. It involved the transfer of practical skills, as well as the instillment of moral values and transference of an appreciation and understanding of community history and customs.

In the book *Education in Africa*, Nigerian historian A. Babs Fafunwa identifies seven "cardinal goals" of traditional African education:

- ✳ To develop the child's latent physical skills.
- ✳ To develop character.
- ✳ To inculcate respect for elders and those in positions of authority.
- ✳ To develop intellectual skills.
- ✳ To acquire specific vocational training and to develop a healthy attitude towards honest labor.
- ✳ To develop a sense of belonging and to encourage active participation in family and community affairs.
- ✳ To understand, appreciate, and promote the cultural heritage of the community at large.

The methods used in indigenous education were experiential, meaning that children observed, imitated, and participated in physical activity. For example, indigenous education might include dancing, playing a musical instrument, planting and harvesting crops, or weaving. Education was connected to daily life. Many of the educational activities contributed to the economic health of the community.

There was a vocational aspect to indigenous education, with attention to agriculture, crafts, or professions. Apprenticeships were common in a wide range of vocations, including traditional medicine, pottery making, fishing, and drumming. The nature of the education depended on the society's needs and the status of the child. The content was integrated, not separated into subject areas. Therefore, children learned the geography of their surroundings at the same time that they learned the history. Education was developmentally appropriate, aligning with the level of physical and mental maturity of the children.

A close link existed between traditional education and social life. Children acquired competencies through participation in community activities. Where societies had a strong oral tradition, education would include storytelling, songs of praise, greetings for various occasions, and proverbs.

As with most societies, in Africa traditional education first took place in the home, with parents serving as the child's first educators (this continues to be true today). Grandparents, aunts, and uncles often played important roles in educating children after the age of four. Generally it was the older family and community members who passed along the history of the family, clan, and larger society. The wider community also had responsibilities for educating youth. Elders taught by their words and by their example. In some African societies, peer groups formed the basis for traditional education.

When foreigners, such as missionaries and colonial officers, viewed indigenous education systems in Africa, they judged them as "backward." Perhaps this is because traditional education systems did not resemble the systems of Europe, which were more formal and visibly structured.

THE INFLUENCE OF RELIGIOUS EDUCATION MODELS: ISLAM AND CHRISTIANITY

Christian and Islamic missionaries both placed great value on education to support their evangelistic activities. In many West and East African countries, Islam predates Christian evangelism. Islam spread from Arab North Africa to West Africa, where it helped to shape education systems and culture. Today the majority of African countries have significant Islamic influence.

Islamic training focused on knowledge of the Qur'an (also spelled Koran), the religion's holy scriptures; the traditions of the Prophet (Hadith); and the canon law of Islam (Shari'a). Qur'anic schools were located in a variety of settings, including mosques, private houses, and custom buildings.

Children as young as three began their education in the Qur'an by memorizing verses and reciting them in chorus in a specific style. From there, students moved on to learn the Arabic alphabet of 26 letters. They needed to be able to recognize the letters, pronounce them, and write them. By the end of this first level of education, the *kuttab*, students started to read. At the next level, the curriculum was more complex. It focused on understanding the meaning of the verses that were memorized. Instruction was given in a local language to enhance students' understanding. The third level of Qur'anic education focused on grammar, usually learned by rote. Those who went on to the university level chose a specialization and studied at an Islamic university or with local specialists at home. These students read Arabic writings of earlier scholars. Completion of this stage granted the student a license for teaching.

Qur'anic schools were open Saturday through Wednesday and were not as formal as Christian or colonial government schools. Tremendous variation existed across Qur'anic schools. There were few rules, and memorization of the Qur'an was the only common thread. Classes included students of different ages, and students moved on when they mastered the material. Peer tutoring was used; older students often helped younger ones. Fees were sometimes paid in cash and sometimes in goods such as food, cloth, or prayer mats. The amount varied between teachers. Apart from paying fees, students were expected to help their teachers in various activities, such as setting up for an event or performing plays at religious festivals.

The qualifications of teachers ranged widely. Some teachers were highly trained scholars; others could only recite Qur'anic verses and write the Arabic alphabet. Those known as *ulama*

In Omdurman, Sudan, Muslim schoolboys read and recite Qur'anic verses written on wooden tablets. The only textbook used in Islamic primary school is the Qur'an, and typically the teacher has the only actual copy. When they move on to secondary school, the students will learn Arabic grammar and read interpretations of the verses they have memorized.

were high-status members of a community and were considered very learned individuals.

Christian missionaries introduced formal schooling with the aim of developing literacy skills sufficient to read the Bible. Further education was designed to train local teachers and pastors in order to support the evangelical mission. There was a heavy emphasis on morality and standards of behavior. Obedience, order, honesty, and sobriety were stressed over academic skills.

Within the classroom, the teaching methods were authoritarian and generally called for the students to be obedient and passive. Students were not allowed to do independent work. Classrooms were highly structured, with rows of seats and a teacher at the front of the room. Children were grouped by age level.

The curriculum in the missionary schools was disconnected from village life and often aimed to alienate children from their African culture and value system. Unlike indigenous education, formal schooling under missionaries (and colonial governments) was not part of economic life. It produced nothing of value to the family or community.

Missionaries generally did not coordinate their educational work. Each mission focused on the territory in which it operated and paid no attention to the needs beyond that location. The social mobility of Africans was not a concern.

Even among missions of the same religious denomination, education varied. The Portuguese Catholic missions in Mozambique, using Portuguese as the sole language of instruction and relying on rote learning methods, emphasized the catechism. In other parts of Africa, education at Catholic missions stressed social justice.

COLONIALISM AND EDUCATION

The colonial experience had significant direct impact on the education systems of almost all African countries, and that impact is still evident today, decades after independence. Even in the few African countries that were never colonized, education systems experienced external influence in one of three ways: occupation (Ethiopia was occupied by Italy in 1935–1941); migration (Liberia was created by freed slaves from the United States); or proximity to colonial regimes in surrounding territories. While seven European colonial powers (Belgium, Britain, the Netherlands, France, Germany, Portugal, and Spain) operated on the continent, France and Britain left the greatest educational legacy.

The purpose of education under colonial rule was to further colonial interests. Over time, this meant a steady but limited flow of African manpower for colonial enterprises. Africans were given access to the minimum education necessary to fulfill the requirements of positions allowed by the colonial government. These included laborers for European-owned farms and mines, clerks in the colonial administration, interpreters, preachers, and teachers. All the colonial powers had school systems divided into primary, secondary, and university levels. Primary schools were few, but secondary schools were even fewer. Usually secondary schools had boarding facilities, as most of the students lived too far away to walk each day. All schools required fees.

THE LEGACY OF BRITISH COLONIAL EDUCATION ON AFRICA

Despite these commonalities, there were significant differences across colonial education models. The European colonial powers differed in the content, length, and volume of education they afforded to Africans. There were differences in long-term visions for the colonies; the British recognized and prepared for the likelihood of self-rule before the French. The 1925 report of the Phelps-Stokes Commission on African Education in British Colonies argued that the colonial education system should conserve the social fabric of the various peoples of Africa and adapt education to the colonial circumstances. Consequently, British colonial administrations sought to alter schooling to fit the local context. They also expanded secondary and higher education opportunities for Africans. Vocational training was promoted over academic training; however, the labor market was not opened for Africans, so academic education continued to be the path to salaried jobs. Higher education institutions were established in the colonies with oversight by British universities and, from 1946, the Inter-University Council for Higher Education in the Colonies.

British colonial rule established a racially segregated education system in some colonies, including Kenya and Tanzania. There were separate schools for Africans, Asians (usually of Indian descent), and Europeans, but there was no uniformity in standards or facilities across the racial systems. Unsurprisingly, the African schools were the least endowed with resources.

In northern Nigeria, the British applied indirect rule, allowing the Qur'anic schools to expand while officially supporting Christian education in the south. This led to an imbalance in formal educational opportunities in Nigeria.

The British government decentralized education in the colonies to the colonial territorial departments and later to regional and municipal bodies. Schools run by missions and other voluntary organizations pressured the colonial government for financial support. As a result, a system of grants-in-aid developed from 1870 onward through which non-governmental schools received financial support. In return, the colonial government had some supervision and inspection power. Schools not receiving colonial government support were run privately and relied entirely on private contributions.

When the British took over responsibility for administering Tanganyika as a United Nations Trust Territory, a new policy of "Education for Adaptation" was established, which aimed to combine Western and African values. After World War II the racial differences in educational opportunities became more striking. The new "Education for Modernization" approach, with greater post-primary opportunities, was open to Europeans, Asians, and only a few Africans. The majority of Africans attended rural schools with a vocational/agricultural curriculum taught in Swahili. Few options existed past primary schooling. At the time of independence in 1961, Tanzania had only 176 upper-secondary graduates, although it had a population of 10.5 million.

From as early as 1929, Africans pressured colonial governments to provide more and better schools. In British colonies there was local community action for education, including the opening of schools. In Kenya the Kikuyu Independent Schools Association was established in 1929 to advocate for better schooling conditions. In Ghana the United Gold Coast Convention called for greater educational opportunities for Africans. In Nigeria ethnically based unions, such as the Ibo Union, called for improved education as well as a greater political voice. Various groups offered scholarships for children of their members to study at universities overseas. This type of community involvement was not common in French colonial Africa, where a French Colonial Office scholarship to study in Paris remained the height of the educational pyramid.

THE LEGACY OF FRENCH ASSIMILATION ON AFRICAN EDUCATION

Colonial education often meant trying to alienate Africans from their culture. This was particularly the case for the French colonial government, which saw its colonies as offshore units of France. Indigenous education was seen as backward and was rejected, if not banned. The French colonial education system aimed to replicate the education system in France and, in the process, denigrated African cultures. The curriculum, like the colonial philosophy, was of acculturation. This meant that schooling aimed to replace African cultural systems with French systems. The curriculum in French colonial schools, dictated from Paris, was the same as the curriculum for French school-children. It was taught in French and included reciting French poems, reading French literature, and studying French geography and history. The curriculum was academic, with no attention to such practical subjects as agriculture. At the secondary level French teachers often taught in African schools.

In French colonial Africa, where the authorities viewed schooling only as a means to prepare a small number of Africans to fill the limited clerical positions in the colonial administration, access to primary education was very restricted. Access to

In this 1958 photo, a French missionary poses with children near Brazzaville in what is now the Republic of Congo.

higher levels of education in Francophone Africa was also extremely limited, since providing a French schooling experience was expensive. France aimed to create a small African aristocracy devoted to French culture and way of life—a goal that necessitated limited availability.

In French colonies, missionaries were actively supported by the colonial administrations. Tensions arose between Christians and Muslims over the favoritism shown toward Christian churches and schools by colonial administrations.

Secular, or nonreligious, schools were not introduced on the continent until the late 19th and early 20th centuries. The focus

In Mali, Dogon schoolchildren learn to speak, read, and write in French. These children write answers to questions on small chalkboards and then hold them up to be checked. The native Dogon language has many variants, some of which are so different that speakers cannot understand one another. Among the Dogon, French is considered necessary for social advancement.

continued to be on religious education, but the curriculum became examination driven.

The French government was late in recognizing the need for higher education institutions in its colonies. Before World War II it had promoted higher education in France as the best option for the very small African elite that reached postsecondary levels. Starting in the 1950s France established overseas branches of French universities.

OTHER EUROPEAN COLONIAL INFLUENCES

The Germans generally left education in their colonies to missionaries. German administrations did, however, exercise influence to ensure that the kind of training available to Africans served the needs of those in power (namely, by guaranteeing a supply of servants and laborers). In the German colonies, the education of Africans was intended to keep Africans inferior, and, in the words of one observer, to avoid inculcating "such mischievous and intolerable ideas as democracy, the brotherhood of man . . . human freedom and the like." In Tanganyika the Germans introduced secular schools in the 1890s.

The Belgians, controlling the Belgian Congo, Rwanda, and Burundi, made little effort to train Africans. Instead they left the task of education mainly to Catholic missionaries, who focused on religious training for the priesthood and vocational training. A university was established in Kinshasa as an overseas campus of the Catholic University of Louvain.

The Portuguese followed a similar path to the French, providing educational opportunities to very few in the colonies of Angola, Mozambique, Guinea-Bissau, São Tomé and Príncipe, and Cape Verde. Under the colonial education policies of António de Oliveira Salazar, the Portuguese dictator, educational opportunities deteriorated further for Africans. In 1966, 90 percent of the

African population in Mozambique was illiterate (as were 4 in 10 Portuguese settlers).

Ethiopia, which was only briefly under the control of foreigners, still chose to follow a European model for its education system. English or French served as the language of instruction, and textbooks were purchased from the United States and United Kingdom. The link between the monarchy and the Christian church meant that the curriculum had a Christian bias. During the Italian occupation beginning in 1935, education suffered as schools were destroyed and many educated Ethiopians killed. In rebuilding the education system after World War II, the Ethiopian government found itself dependent on foreign teachers who taught in English. The government's inability to pay foreign teachers eventually helped lead, in 1955, to the adoption of a native tongue, Amharic (spoken in north-central Ethiopia), as the main language of instruction. But Christian bias in the teaching force and curriculum led to tensions between Ethiopia's Christian and Muslim communities.

As the European colonial powers began withdrawing from Africa in the late 1950s and the continent approached the independence period, school enrollment rates were low overall and even lower for girls. In 1956 Guinea, which would earn independence two years later, had less than 10 percent of its school-aged children in schools, and only a quarter of those were female. Girls made up one-third of the 25 percent enrolled in Tanzania in 1960. And in Ethiopia overall enrollment was just 5 percent, with females constituting one-quarter of that group. Throughout the continent adult literacy rates were low.

APARTHEID EDUCATION

A special situation existed in the southern African countries of Namibia and South Africa prior to 1990. The South African government assumed control of Namibia (then called South West

Ethiopia was briefly occupied by Italy beginning in 1935. Even the country's short exposure to European influence left lasting impressions on its way of life. Debts incurred from rebuilding after the occupation set Ethiopia back economically and left the education system struggling for money.

Africa) in 1920 under a League of Nations mandate. However, South Africa went beyond its mandate and illegally occupied the territory. Little was done to expand educational opportunities for Africans. The first state school for Africans in Namibia was not established until 1935. There were no state schools in the north of the country, where most of the population resided, until after 1960. And the limited schooling that was available was of short duration, usually only five years. Despite the presence of hundreds of mission schools, no African pupil completed grade 12 until 1948.

In the 1950s South Africa developed the system of apartheid, which supported the separation of races and a racial hierarchy. The Bantu Education Act of 1953 translated the policy for education. The apartheid regime took over the administration of schools in South Africa and Namibia, rejecting missionary education. Arguing that it was adapting education for African conditions, the South African government promoted the subservience and subjugation of Africans while teaching racial bigotry. Apartheid schooling proved to be the antithesis of genuine education, imprisoning rather than liberating minds. At the time of Namibia's independence in 1990, per pupil expenditures in the Administration for Whites were eight times that of the education authority running schools for the largest African ethnic group, the Owambo.

As this sign on a beach near Cape Town suggests, apartheid enforced segregation of the races in South Africa. Under the policy, the White minority enjoyed a disproportionate share of the country's resources in all areas, including education.

SUMMARY

The independence period for sub-Saharan Africa is generally considered to extend from 1957, when Ghana achieved independence, to 1975, when Mozambique and the Comoro Islands celebrated their freedom. After gaining independence from the European colonial powers, African countries had the opportunity to reform their education systems to better fit their needs. These efforts had mixed results.

4 POST-INDEPENDENCE EDUCATIONAL EXPANSION

Following the independence period, African countries experienced great expansion of their education systems as well as substantive changes to the curriculum. One country in particular, Tanzania, is worthy of focus for its experience in redefining the purpose of schooling through its philosophy of "Education for Self-Reliance."

CURRICULAR CHANGES AFTER INDEPENDENCE

Many countries pursued a reform of the curriculum referred to as "Africanization." This entailed the revision of curricular offerings, syllabi, teaching and learning materials, examination systems, and other resources. The aim was to have the education system reflect African values, identities, and perspectives rather than those of the former colonial powers. New curricula became a way to promote national identity and to politically socialize the next generation of citizens. Social studies textbooks, in particular,

(Opposite) Senegalese authors wrote the books being used in this Dakar classroom. In the post-independence period, many African school systems have revised the curriculum to focus more on African history, values, and cultural accomplishments.

were rewritten to recognize African history and the struggles for independence. The language arts curriculum was changed in many settings to incorporate novels, poetry, and plays by African writers.

The choice of language for instruction was often political, and some countries abandoned the language of the colonial power for an African one. For example, Botswana moved to Setswana for the first four years of instruction, and Tanzania introduced Swahili as the language of instruction.

EXPANSION OF OPPORTUNITIES

During the 1960s newly independent countries across the continent greatly expanded educational opportunities. This expansion—which involved both creating more space in schools and eliminating barriers to school attendance—was driven by popular demand and political and national imperatives. There was tremendous unmet demand for education, since schooling had

become the major path by which people could rise in society and gain access to salaried positions. In the run-up to independence, nationalist movements promised expanded educational opportunities, and their legitimacy as new governments was enhanced by delivering on this promise. Furthermore, countries needed educated workers to fill positions that were left by colonial officials or created by expanding economies.

PRIMARY ENROLLMENT

Participation in primary schooling increased significantly between the mid-1960s and the early 1980s. For sub-Saharan Africa as a whole, the primary-school gross enrollment ratio (GER)—the number of children attending primary school (whether of primary school age or not) divided by the number of primary-school-age children in the population—nearly doubled in the 15-year period 1965–1980.

As a statement of their commitment, several African governments established free and compulsory primary education. In 1971 Kenya eliminated primary school fees in regions that were educationally disadvantaged and then extended the policy to the

	TABLE 4 PRIMARY AND SECONDARY GROSS ENROLLMENT RATIO (GER)[a] IN SUB-SAHARAN AFRICA, 1965–1980			
	PRIMARY GER		**SECONDARY GER**	
	1965	1980	1965	1980
Total	41	79	4	16
Male	52	87	6	21
Female	30	67	2	10

a.   School enrollment as a percentage of the relevant age group. Data are weighted for each country's
     share with aggregate population.
Source: World Bank 1989.

whole country in 1974. In Botswana primary education is free but not compulsory.

SECONDARY SCHOOLING

Secondary school enrollments in sub-Saharan Africa also increased between 1965 and 1980, but the overall rates remained much lower than the rates for attendance in primary school. By 1980 secondary school students represented 16 percent of all children of secondary school age. Although still a low GER, this figure had quadrupled since 1965.

Colonial secondary schools had typically been boarding schools, which are much more expensive than day schools to build and operate. After gaining independence, many countries constructed only day secondary schools and started converting secondary boarding schools to day schools.

Two patterns are evident in the enrollment ratio data for sub-Saharan Africa's largest states from the mid-1960s to the mid-1980s, as Table 5 shows. The countries, which combined are home to more than half of sub-Saharan Africa's people, represent six of the seven most populous nations in the region. (South Africa is excluded because no data was available until 1990.) The first trend is the significant increase in primary and secondary enrollment for each of the countries between 1965 and 1980. Nigeria, Zaire (now the Democratic Republic of the Congo), Tanzania, and Kenya all approached universal primary education, while in Ethiopia and Sudan primary enrollments grew to 35 percent and 50 percent, respectively. At the secondary level, the Democratic Republic of the Congo experienced the greatest increase, with enrollment rising to 35 percent in 1980. While the other five countries expanded secondary enrollment, opportunities remained available for less than one-fifth of the school-age population.

The second trend is the decline in primary enrollment rates after 1980. Overall, sub-Saharan Africa's GER for primary school declined by 6 percent between 1980 and 1986. Tanzania's GER declined by 24 percent, and Kenya's by 16 percent. At the secondary level, participation rates either stagnated or continued to increase in the 1980s.

			PRIMARY GER[2]			SECONDARY GER[2]		
COUNTRY	**2003 POPULATION IN THOUSANDS**[1]	**% OF SUB-SAHARAN AFRICA'S POPULATION**	**1965**	**1980**	**1986**	**1965**	**1980**	**1986**
Sub-Saharan Africa	665,496	--	41	79	73	4	16	20
Nigeria	124,009	18.63%	32	97	--	5	19	--
Ethiopia	70,698	10.62%	11	35	36	2	9	12
Zaire (now Dem. Rep. of Congo)	52,771	7.93%	70	98	--	5	35	--
United Republic of Tanzania	36,977	5.56%	32	93	69	2	3	3
Sudan	33,610	5.05%	29	50	50	4	16	20
Kenya	31,987	4.81%	54	110	94	4	19	20
Sub-total (weighted)	350,032	52.60%	34	82	69	4	17	21

TABLE 5
EDUCATION EXPANSION IN THE SIX MOST POPULOUS SUB-SAHARAN AFRICAN COUNTRIES, 1965–1986

Source: (1) UNICEF *State of the World's Children 2005*. (2) World Bank 1989.

HIGHER EDUCATION

At the end of colonial rule, African universities typically served a small segment of the population. They used the language of the colonizer for instruction and had limited curriculum offerings, emphasizing liberal arts and the humanities rather than science and technology. In most of the countries of British colonial Africa, university-level education was available, but it was linked to British institutions, often as the degree-granting institution. The independence period saw the de-linking of African universities from colonial affiliates. Some countries established new institutions, while others transformed existing ones. In the early 1960s the University of East Africa was established with constituent colleges in Kenya (Royal University College), Tanzania (University College of Dar es Salaam), and Uganda (Makerere University College). This federation lasted until the collapse of the East African Community in 1977. The member colleges were renamed as independent universities, dropping their "college" label.

After gaining independence, many former French colonies supported keeping the strong links with French universities, even when the African universities became nationalized. France continued to finance these institutions, in many cases until the 1970s, and this delayed the Africanization of the personnel and curriculum. The Portuguese colonies had no universities until the 1960s, and even then the universities in Angola and

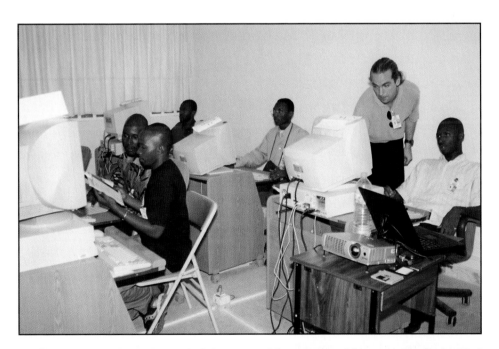

In 2002 the University of Kankan in Guinea opened its computer lab, connecting the isolated institution to the Internet. There are three computer labs, like the one pictured here, across the campus.

Mozambique served Portuguese settlers, not Africans. In 1976, a year after its independence, Mozambique changed the name of its sole university to Eduardo Mondlane University. Guinea-Bissau and São Tomé and Príncipe do not have universities. The former Belgian colonies of Rwanda and Burundi each established national universities, the University of Burundi in 1960 and the National University of Rwanda in 1963.

Across the continent, the colonial model remained the standard for quality. But the United States higher education model started to have some influence.

ADULT LITERACY EDUCATION

Adult education programs serve adults (usually defined as 15 years or older) who left school early or never attended school at all. Adult literacy education is the main form of education available to adults in Africa. Beyond literacy education, other forms of adult education include agricultural extension, community development programs, and industrial or vocational training. Adult education, particularly literacy training, is often referred to as nonformal education.

Progress has been made in reducing illiteracy rates in Africa, but high population growth has meant that in absolute numbers illiteracy has been increasing since the independence period. Illiteracy is higher among women than men.

Language choice for literacy education is a complex and political issue. By necessity, materials appropriate for adult learners must be developed in local languages, and this is very costly. Many governments allocate minuscule amounts of the education budget to adult literacy.

Literacy programs vary considerably in their focus and content. Some focus on economic production skills, especially agriculture or health care. Others focus on the political and emancipatory purposes of literacy, aiming to empower adults to be active and

TABLE 6
NUMBER OF ADULT ILLITERATES (MILLIONS) AND ILLITERACY RATES IN SUB-SAHARAN AFRICA, 1970–2010

YEAR	NUMBER OF ILLITERATES	ILLITERACY RATE
1980	--	61 %
1985[1]	133.6	59.1 %
1990[1]	138.8	52.7 %
2000–10 [2]	139.7	39.6 %

Source: (1) UNESCO, quoted in Okedara 1994. (2) UIS Database, 2012.

effective citizens and community members. Some organizations in specific economic sectors, such as mining or fishing, promote literacy for a more productive workforce.

REDEFINING THE PURPOSE OF EDUCATION: THE TANZANIAN EXPERIMENT

After Tanzania gained independence in 1961, its leaders were strongly influenced by theories of modernization, believing that the transition from an agrarian economy to an industrialized one would bring about economic growth and development. Tanzania's economy at independence largely revolved around small-scale agriculture, with 90 percent of the labor force employed in farming. Consequently, Tanzania's First Development Plan favored capital-intensive industry and commercial farms for the growing of export crops such as coffee, tea, and sisal. The plan ignored rural areas and limited industry to a few urban centers rather than spreading it throughout the country. The "modern" economy of banks, insurance companies, industry, and commercial farms was mostly foreign owned.

In 1961 Tanzania—with a population of 10.5 million—had only 100 university graduates and fewer than 200 upper-secondary-school graduates. Moreover, 75 percent of the adult population was illiterate. Clearly the expansion of educational opportunities had to become a major priority. The racially based three-tier system for Europeans, Asians, and Africans was abolished, and schools were opened to all races. The curriculum was made more relevant, and Swahili was introduced as the language of instruction, largely to help unite the country's 120 ethnic groups.

By the mid-1960s, however, it became obvious that Tanzania was not going to reach its development goals if it continued to follow the same course. In 1967 President Julius Nyerere issued his statement of social philosophy, the Arusha Declaration, and the government started on a path of African socialism and self-reliance. This experiment involved rethinking many aspects of Tanzanian society, including its education system. The same year that Nyerere issued the Arusha Declaration, he released the policy statement "Education for Self-Reliance," in which he asked the large, philosophical question: What is the purpose of education? In the essay, Nyerere also posed three key practical questions:

✳ What kind of society are we trying to build?
✳ What's wrong with the present system?
✳ Can we correct these faults in the education system? How?

In answer to the first question, Nyerere reiterated his vision of African socialism for Tanzania. He acknowledged that, in his predominantly rural country, most citizens would never be educated beyond the primary level. "These are the economic facts of life for our country," Nyerere wrote. "They are the practical meaning of our poverty."

His analysis of what was wrong with the country's education system identified a mismatch between the colonial model of education and the needs of independent Tanzania. Nyerere argued that Tanzania's existing education system was designed for a colonialist and capitalist society and, therefore, was elitist. The system labeled the 87 percent of the children who did not go on to secondary school as "failures" and developed a sense of superiority in those who "succeeded." He argued that the education system, especially secondary schools, divorced students from the society for which it was supposed to prepare them. Tanzania's schools promoted the idea that only knowledge from books or "educated people" was worth knowing, ignoring attitudes, character, traditional knowledge, and wisdom from experience. Students needed to learn as they worked and not be protected from hard work, Nyerere argued. The curriculum privileged white-collar skills and raised unrealistic expectations about graduates' gaining salaried jobs. The education system encouraged individualistic instincts, rather than cooperative ones, and defined social merit as possession of individual

Tanzanian president Julius Nyerere (shown here on his 75th birthday) instituted education initiatives in his country that dramatically increased literacy. Eventually, the country could no longer support its education program financially, and expenditures had to be cut, but Tanzania continues to have an adult literacy rate of nearly 70 percent.

material wealth. Finally, Nyerere maintained, Tanzania's education system introduced attitudes of human inequality, which promoted the domination of the weak by the strong.

Nyerere laid out a vision of how education could be reorganized to serve the community as a whole rather than individual

JULIUS KAMBARAGE NYERERE
(1922–1999)

Julius Nyerere, the first president of Tanzania, became one of Africa's most respected leaders. He was known internationally as *Mwalimu* (Swahili for "teacher") because of his lifelong commitment to education as well as his talents as a secondary school teacher, philosopher, and scholar.

As president of the nationalist political party, the Tanganyika African National Union, Nyerere helped guide his country's peaceful transition to independence from Britain in 1961. He oversaw the union of Tanganyika and Zanzibar and became the first president of the new United Republic of Tanzania in 1964. He was repeatedly reelected and eventually left office voluntarily in 1985.

Nyerere saw an urgent need to improve the lives of Tanzanians. He promoted African socialism and self-reliance, laying out his vision in the 1967 Arusha Declaration. In stressing the urgency and immensity of the problem, he was known to say, "We must run while others walk." The goals of Tanzania's ideology of *ujamaa* were indigenous initiative and control, the elimination of inequalities, state control of the means of production (such as industry), and the maintenance of control over decision making in foreign assistance. Nyerere argued for three values: equality and respect for human dignity; sharing of the resources that are produced by human effort; and work by everyone and exploitation by none. Nyerere believed in the transformative power of literacy and supported the expansion of primary education and national literacy campaigns.

interests. "[T]he only true justification for secondary education," he argued, "is that it is needed by the few for service to the many. . . . There can be no other justification for taxing the many to give education to only a few."

Nyerere's new vision called for a change in the content of the curriculum to prepare students for life and service in the villages and rural areas. The schools were to be reorganized as economic, social, and educational communities that practiced self-reliance. A school farm or workshop would be an integral, contributing part of the institution. Students would be expected to participate in the

Nyerere was a staunch pan-Africanist and was very involved in liberation movements throughout the continent. He was a keynote speaker at the June 1959 meeting in London at which the Boycott South Africa Movement, later renamed the Anti-Apartheid Movement, was launched. Tanzania hosted the African Liberation Committee from its inception in 1963, and Nyerere was a founding father of the Organization of African Unity (OAU). He offered sanctuary in Tanzania to members of African liberation movements from South Africa, Zimbabwe, Mozambique, Angola, and Uganda. Tanzania gave land and other assistance to the African National Congress of South Africa for its headquarters in Morogoro and for the Solomon Mahlangu school. He was a key player in the 1979 Lancaster House conference over Zimbabwe's future. In 1979 Nyerere took the courageous step of sending troops into Uganda after that country's longtime dictator, Idi Amin, had launched an invasion of northwestern Tanzania. The move succeeded in ousting the brutal Amin that same year.

As a scholar, Nyerere wrote many books on African liberation, development, socialism, and education. He translated Shakespeare's *Julius Caesar* and *The Merchant of Venice* into Swahili. After retiring in 1985, Nyerere spent his time farming and engaging in diplomacy in the region. He mediated an end to the civil war in Burundi and served as chairman of the South Commission (later the South Centre), an independent international organization advising on development strategy for developing countries. He established the Mwalimu Nyerere Foundation to continue his work and legacy of peace, unity, and people-centered development. He lived as modestly in retirement as he had as a public servant. In 1999 he died at age 77 from leukemia.

provision of their education by cooking, cleaning, maintaining school grounds, and helping make educational decisions. The school calendar would be more flexible so pupils could participate in productive village activities at home. Attention was to be taken away from examinations and international standards and turned toward new assessments based on student work done for the school and community. As a result of these changes, Nyerere argued, students would develop inquiring minds and gain the basic confidence to be free and equal members of society who valued others not for what they had obtained, but for what they contributed.

In enacting the vision of Education for Self-Reliance, Nyerere sought to make access to primary education more equitable. The government increased the national budget for education, and local and regional governments also invested funds. Every village was given a chance to have a primary school. The grade 4 examination was abolished, thus allowing all pupils who were in primary school to complete the primary cycle. Private primary schools were nationalized, giving the government control and responsibility for all primary schools. Teacher training colleges expanded. The growth in enrollments was phenomenal, and by 1981 the primary gross enrollment ratio was 97 percent.

In addition to the striking gains in primary education, Tanzania achieved a dramatic reduction in illiteracy through a series of adult literacy campaigns. In fact, Tanzania made greater

As part of a literacy campaign in Guinea, this woman learns basic reading and writing skills in order to qualify for a microloan. The combination will enable her to start her own small business.

progress than any other African country in reducing national illiteracy rates during the post-independence period. It used an integrated approach that included significant and sustained funding (Tanzania allocated 10 percent of its national budget to adult literacy); free learning materials; radio broadcasts in support of literacy activities; eyeglasses for adults with poor sight; post-literacy materials in rural areas; continuing education opportunities for literacy graduates; and training of adult literacy educators and administrators. For other African countries wishing to duplicate Tanzania's success, the lesson was clear: progress requires political will, funding, infrastructure to support adult education, and sustained effort.

President Nyerere's Education for Self-Reliance plan recognized that achieving high rates of secondary education was not a realistic goal in Tanzania. Even considering the lower expectations, however, it might be argued that progress in the provision of secondary schooling was insufficient. While primary school opportunities expanded dramatically, the growth of secondary education was much slower and, as a result, access became increasingly selective. The government more than doubled the number of secondary school seats between 1961 and 1980 (from

TABLE 7
TANZANIA ADULT ILLITERACY RATES

YEAR	ADULT ILLITERACY RATE
1967	69%
1975	30%
1977	27%
1981	21%
1983	15%
1986	9.6%

Source: Samoff 1990.

4,196 to 8,913), but since the number of primary school graduates was doubling every five years, a decreasing percentage found places in secondary schools. Despite its *ujamaa* (family) socialist policies, the government allowed private schools to expand to help fill the gap, thus permitting access to be determined by location and relative wealth. By 1985, 46.1 percent of all secondary school students were enrolled in private schools. Yet even with the expansion of private secondary schools, only 5.3 percent of the 1985 primary school graduates were selected for any secondary school, public or private. This was a far cry from the 21.8 percent that were able to enroll in 1961.

Nonetheless, Tanzania's accomplishments in education—including universal primary education and literacy rates of 85 percent—were undeniable. Unfortunately, beginning around 1980 the country experienced a series of economic strains and setbacks (including a costly war with Uganda, droughts, declining agricultural production, and low foreign exchange earnings). These stresses, combined with an inefficient government bureaucracy and corruption, threatened some of Tanzania's educational gains.

School fees were reintroduced in 1984. Even though the concept of self-reliance was central to Tanzania's national philosophy, the country became increasingly dependent on foreign assistance, and its acceptance of foreign aid projects led to a recurring budget that it could not afford. In 1985 Nyerere spoke about the abandonment of Education for Self-Reliance, citing the conflict between ambition and resource limits.

5 EDUCATION FINANCING CHALLENGES

I n addition to being influenced by historical factors, contemporary African education systems are shaped by the political and economic environment. Clearly, strong political will is necessary for educational advancement of a country, but so too is adequate funding. It is important to examine the sources of education financing and the global and local economic forces that have influenced education in Africa.

EDUCATION FUNDING

Education systems in Africa are financed primarily with government revenue generated through various sources, including taxes. Private funding from individuals and businesses contributes a small but increasing piece to the education financing pie. A third funding source for education in Africa is external foreign assistance, also called foreign aid. This configuration of funding sources, in conjunction with other factors, affects access to and the quality of education.

A USAID-sponsored program in Senegal provides schoolchildren with new books. Author Fatou Ndiaye Sow assists students in their reading.

Whether an increasing percentage of children enroll in school is determined by many factors. For example, if the population increases, more children must enroll each year to increase the proportion in school. Changes in household income also affect participation rates because families must pay the direct costs of schooling (such as fees, uniforms, and supplies) and the indirect costs (such as loss of the child's labor). If a family's income declines, parents may need children to stay out of school to work. Public expenditure levels for primary schooling also affect enrollment rates because public funding allows the building of schools, the hiring of teachers, and the purchasing of various learning and teaching resources, such as textbooks and workbooks.

PUBLIC EXPENDITURES IN EDUCATION

From 1970 to 1995, sub-Saharan African governments spent between 15 percent and 17.6 percent of their budgets on education. Even through the difficult economic period of the 1980s, government commitment remained high. In 2000–2001 most of the 17 countries reporting claimed that education spending was between 12 percent and 25.6 percent of total government expenditures. Seven countries spent more than 20 percent on education, with Guinea and Botswana topping the list at 25.6 percent.

Another common way of tracking governments' financial commitment to education is to measure education expenditures as a percentage of gross national product (GNP), which is the total value of goods and services produced annually by a country's nationals (including profits from overseas ventures). In the past, the proportion of GNP that sub-Saharan African nations spent on education was comparable to the rates in North American and European countries (5.1 percent in 1980 and 5.6 percent in 1995). In the early 2000s, public expenditures on education as a percentage of GNP declined in sub-Saharan Africa, possibly because of increased external debt payments. may explain the declining proportion of GNP available for education.

Currently, rates of education spending in sub-Saharan Africa are similar to those of Latin America and the Caribbean, as Table 8 shows. Spending is higher only in North America and Western Europe (5.7 percent).

Breaking down education spending, Table 9 compares government expenditures on primary education across regions of the world, using several African countries as illustrations. These figures are for expenses that recur each year, such as teacher salaries, administrative costs, and utilities. Expenditures for one-time costs, such as construction of new school buildings, are listed in the development (or capital) budget, which is usually a much smaller budget than the recurrent one. The second column suggests that the African countries listed are spending a higher proportion of their recurrent budget on primary education than are other regions as a whole. In addition, teachers' salaries make up almost the entire recurrent expenditure at the primary level.

These expenditure measures have some limitations. The expenditure per pupil indicator does not truly measure quality, and the cost of providing the same quality of education varies

TABLE 8
TOTAL PUBLIC EXPENDITURE ON EDUCATION AS % OF GNP

REGION[1]	TOTAL PUBLIC EXPENDITURE ON EDUCATION AS % OF GNP
Sub-Saharan Africa	5.0
Central Asia	3.2
South & West Asia	3.6
Arab States	4.5
East Asia & Pacific	4.7
Central & Eastern Europe	4.9
Latin America & the Caribbean	5.0
North America & Western Europe	5.7

(1) All values are medians.
Source: UNESCO *EFA Global Monitoring Report 2008*, p. 142.

across and within regions. For example, it costs more to deliver books to a school in northern Nigeria than to deliver them across town from the warehouse in Lagos. Nonetheless, the indicators provide a helpful means by which to compare public financing of education in sub-Saharan Africa and the rest of the world.

IMPACT OF ECONOMIC DECLINE ON EDUCATION

In the 1980s and 1990s African governments faced poor terms of trade and experienced declines in agricultural production due to drought and political instability (much of which, in southern Africa, was fomented by South Africa's apartheid regime). During these decades, many African countries adopted Structural Adjustment Programs, loans that carried International Monetary Fund (IMF) requirements for the liberalization of economies. Among the conditions for the loans was the reduction of government spending in the social sectors of health and education. While African governments maintained their commitment to education, the overall funding levels declined. The impact was felt on African education systems in several ways. During this period, teacher salaries could not keep pace with inflation, so teachers took second or even third jobs, resulting in less time at school. With no money for new school buildings or new teachers, governments could not sustain the expansion of the previous two decades. Class sizes remained large, making classes more difficult to teach. Without mainte-nance, buildings deteriorated, and curriculum and textbook revi-sion slowed to a crawl. Schools went years without getting new

TABLE 9
ESTIMATED PUBLIC RECURRENT EXPENDITURE ON PRIMARY EDUCATION FOR SELECTED AFRICAN COUNTRIES AND WORLD REGIONS

REGION	PUBLIC RECURRENT EXPENDITURE ON PRIMARY EDUCATION AS % OF PUBLIC RECURRENT EXPENDITURE ON EDUCATION	PRIMARY TEACHERS' SALARIES AS % OF PUBLIC RECURRENT EXPENDITURE ON PRIMARY EDUCATION
Sub-Saharan Africa[1]		
Côte d'Ivoire	43.4	83.2
Lesotho	46.7	92.3
Namibia	59.4	91.4
South Africa	47.9	90.2
Togo	44.2	84.3
East Asia & Pacific	43.5	--
Latin America & Caribbean	38.7	--
North America & Western Europe	27.4	--

(1) Data not available for sub-Saharan Africa as a whole or other regions not included above.
Source: UNESCO *EFA Global Monitoring Report 2005*, Table 14.

materials, and teachers rarely received professional development training. In Malawi, for example, teachers complained that once they were assigned to a school they were "posted and forgotten."

"User fees" were encouraged by the World Bank in an attempt to make up for declining government funding. However, with the poor economic situation, household incomes were also declining. The inability of families to pay, combined with the deterioration in the quality of schools, led to stagnation in enrollments throughout the continent. Comoros, Lesotho, Mali, Mozambique, Togo, Tanzania, the Democratic Republic of the Congo, and Zambia experienced declines in primary enrollment from 1980 levels.

(Left) This classroom in rural Zambia has a chalkboard that is so worn it is almost impossible to read. The school, like many in Africa, lacks the money to buy or replace essential materials such as blackboards, desks, and books. (Below) Crowded classrooms, like this one in Uganda, are common in Africa. Learning is more difficult under such conditions.

THE EDUCATION-DEBT CONNECTION

Many argue that Africa's large external debt is crippling the continent's economies because governments must use large percentages of their revenues to pay or "service" those debts. This takes money away from efforts to improve the lives of citizens.

In 1970 Africa's total external debt was just under $11 billion. By 2002 it had soared to $295 billion. Malawi spends between 25 percent and 30 percent of government revenue on debt service. Mauritania, Senegal, Guinea-Bissau, Guinea, and Ghana each spend 15 to 20 percent. With such large portions of government budgets devoted to servicing old debts, less is available for health and education. UNICEF estimates that since the late 1980s as many as 5 million children and vulnerable adults have lost their lives in sub-Saharan Africa as a result of the debt crunch.

Oxfam, an international advocacy and development organization, issued a stern warning in 1998:

> The case for developing the education-debt linkage is only reinforced by the state of education in the world's poorest highly indebted countries. . . . In sub-Saharan Africa, where school enrollment rates are actually falling, 56 million children will be out of school by the year 2000. Millions more will learn little in schools which are often without trained staff and even the most basic equipment and materials. Without a concerted effort to resolve the education and debt crisis in sub-Saharan Africa, the region's political and economic marginalization will continue.

The majority of the world's heavily indebted poor countries are in sub-Saharan Africa. Debt relief and debt cancellation initiatives therefore have significant implications for education in Africa.

PRIVATE FINANCING

Private financing of education may come from either private

sponsorship of schools (usually fees paid by those who attend) or by payments to public schools by private individuals or businesses. Private schools are defined as those controlled and managed, whether for profit or not, by a private body such as a non-governmental organization, religious body, special interest group, foundation, or business enterprise. Private schools are generally more expensive than public schools, although scholarships and fee waivers may be available.

PREVALENCE OF PRIVATE SCHOOLS

Private school data is available only for 35 sub-Saharan African countries. For the countries reporting, private schools represent a small minority of all educational institutions. Yet private schools are by no means insignificant in these countries. At the preprimary level, only about 1 in 10 children in sub-Saharan Africa are enrolled, but most of this enrollment (61.8 percent) is in private preprimary schools. Sub-Saharan Africa has a higher percentage of children enrolled in private primary schools than all other regions of the world except Latin America and the Caribbean region. And, as Table 10 indicates, sub-Saharan Africa ranks fourth among the world's regions in percentage of enrollments at the secondary level.

In order to escape the poor conditions of public schools, many well-off Africans send their children to private schools. Private schools tend to have better equipment and smaller classes.

For sub-Saharan Africa overall, an estimated 9.2 percent of students enrolled at the primary level attend a private school, but

TABLE 10
PRIVATE ENROLLMENT AS %
OF TOTAL ENROLLMENT BY REGION

REGION[1]	PRIMARY EDUCATION	SECONDARY EDUCATION
Sub-Saharan Africa	9.2	13.3
World	7.2	11.7
North America & Western Europe	6.7	8.8
Central & Eastern Europe	0.8	1.1
Central Asia	0.6	0.9
Arab States	7.4	7.6
Latin America & Caribbean	14.7	22.2
East Asia & Pacific	8.2	16.1
South & West Asia	3.8	14.4

(1) All values are medians.
Source: UNESCO *EFA Global Monitoring Report 2005*, Table 14.

rates vary dramatically by country, from Zimbabwe's 87.6 percent to Lesotho's 0.1 percent. Nine countries have at least 20 percent of their primary students in private schools.

Higher education in Africa is primarily government funded, but private institutions are growing because of increased demand, cuts in funding for public institutions, declines in the capacity of public universities, and increased interest by foreign providers. In some countries there are more private than public higher education institutions, though the former enroll far fewer students because they tend to offer specialized training, such as business administration and computer science. Private higher education institutions include religiously based as well as nonsectarian schools, although religious institutions are more likely to offer assistance with fees. Private enrollment is higher in Kenya, which has 13 private colleges and universities,

TABLE 11
SUB-SAHARAN AFRICAN COUNTRIES
WITH THE HIGHEST PRIVATE SCHOOL
ENROLLMENT RATES

PRIMARY LEVEL		SECONDARY LEVEL	
Zimbabwe	87.6	Mauritius	73.3
Togo	40.7	Zimbabwe	71.3
Chad[1]	33.8	Comoros	42.1
Gabon	29.3	Burkina Faso[2]	34.4
Mauritius	24.2	Cameroon	30.5
Congo	23.7	Gabon[2]	29.8
Cameroon	23.5	Senegal	25.2
Madagascar	20.4	Gambia[1]	20.9
Guinea	20.4	Nigeria	20.7

(1) UIS estimate.
(2) 2001 data.
Source: UNESCO Institute for Statistics database.

than in most African countries, but the rate is still only 20 percent. Sudan has 22 private higher education institutions; Ghana, 13; and Togo, 22. Most are located in the main cities to take advantage of the infrastructure and large student pool. Not all private universities meet the standard for government approval. Only in a few cases do private institutions receive government financial support. In many places, the private schools offer a second chance for those who are not admitted to the public universities. Quality, legal status, and cost remain important issues.

SCHOOL FEES

The global Education for All campaign advocates for free primary education in order to expand access for all children. The experience of several countries indicates that when fees are charged for primary school, the most vulnerable children are less likely to attend. These include girls, AIDS orphans, and street children. In January 2003 the recently elected Kenyan government abolished primary school fees, and 1.3 million children entered school for the first time; this represented an increase of 22 percent. In Malawi in 1994, the newly elected government delivered on its campaign promise and provided free primary education. Enrollment increased from 1.9 million to 2.8 million at the start of the 1995 school year. Today the majority of African countries have no fees for primary school, but in most cases fees are charged at all other levels, even by public schools.

There are some good reasons to charge fees. If school fees are abolished but government budget allocations to schools are not increased, a decline in quality can be expected. Primary school fees typically stay at the school, where administrators have discretion about how best to use them, instead of being passed on to higher levels of the government bureaucracy. And there is emerging evidence that school governing bodies are more likely to focus on quality if they have funds to apply to the issue. Furthermore, eliminating official school fees does not necessarily make schooling free: some schools will require parents to purchase supplies that were previously provided to students at no charge, such as textbooks or pens and paper. These unofficial costs will keep some children from school and prevent others who do attend from having the supplies they need for learning. For these reasons, some experts argue that it is better to have an official fee but to cap the amount a school may charge.

Allowing individual schools free rein in setting fees, as is the case in South Africa, typically results in unequal access and quality. Schools with high fees, the experience of South Africa suggests, can indeed make significant improvements in the quality of the educational experience they provide (for example, by hiring additional teachers to cover special subjects or by reduc-

The Kenyan woman in this photo used a microloan to purchase a dairy cow. The proceeds from the milk sales pay for the private school fees for her four children.

ing class sizes). But these schools tend to be located in more affluent urban areas and to draw their students from the families of the well-to-do, who can afford the higher fees. In poor rural areas, schools cannot charge high fees because families would not be able to afford them. Thus the schools are left without sufficient resources to improve the quality of the teaching and learning experience.

EXTERNAL ASSISTANCE

Foreign aid to Africa for education declined sharply in the 1990s, and the poorer African countries were the hardest hit. Even though international aid donors pledged significant increases in support at the 1990 Education for All Conference in Jomtein, Thailand, by 1998 bilateral government-to-government aid for education had actually fallen by 15 percent. European Union grants for education in Africa fell slightly during the 1990s. While the number and value of World Bank loans for basic education and educational projects claiming a gender impact rose globally in the 1990s, loans for education in sub-Saharan Africa declined, both in terms of total value and as a proportion of all World Bank education loans. But the richer African countries tended to get larger loans, amounting to twice the value per capita. And despite the rhetorical commitment to addressing gender inequalities, it was the countries with smaller gender gaps that received more World Bank support. This indicates that there were incentives for donor project managers to claim their project had a gender impact, regardless of the need.

ISSUES OF DEPENDENCE AND EFFECTIVENESS

Even with declining levels, foreign aid played an increasing role in financing education in some countries. In 2012, for example, foreign aid provided over 80 percent of Malawi's development budget and almost one-quarter of the education sector budget.

Yet the effectiveness of foreign aid for education in Africa has been questioned. The three main criticisms are funding agencies' failure to coordinate aid, Africa's increased dependence on aid, and the conditions placed on how governments receiving aid may allocate those resources.

Children in Guinea pose in front of recently constructed classrooms with their new backpacks. Foreign aid helps finance many education projects in Africa, but that assistance, critics say, often creates significant problems in recipient countries.

Most African countries receive aid from at least eight sources, and often the total is much higher. The burden to harmonize and coordinate the different aid programs falls on overstretched government bureaucracies, rather than on the funding governments and organizations. By acting individually, aid agencies are more likely to have their interests and policies served, often at the expense of the priorities of the countries they purport to help.

Additionally, aid can lead to more than just monetary dependence. Many African countries depend on foreign advice, and this has at times kept these countries from developing their own high-level expertise. Believing that any education initiative will require external funding, African decision makers pursue initiatives that they are certain they can get funded, rather than those that are best aligned with national priorities.

The third issue is the conditional, or tied, nature of the aid. Foreign assistance, particularly from international financial institutions like the World Bank, comes with conditions that governments must meet, even if those conditions contradict the national goals of the recipient country. Aid is often tied to the purchase of technical assistance, goods, or services from the donor country. Critics of aid argue that rather than redistributing resources to Africa, aid results in a net outflow of capital and skills back to the funding countries.

HIGHER EDUCATION'S LACK OF SUPPORT

African higher education institutions have been dependent on external support since their founding. In the post-independence period, assistance has come from overseas private philanthropic organizations, foreign governments, aid agencies, foreign scholarly societies, and overseas universities. In the early years of independence, there was considerable aid for a wide range of needs, including building construction, professional development of staff, salaries of local and international staff, library and laboratory acquisitions, and computer purchases. Starting in the late 1960s, the World Bank's focus on education lending in Africa shifted to basic education. Postsecondary education, including the universities, received only about 12 percent of all education lending between 1963 and 1990.

Higher education systems are expensive, and tuition fees cannot cover all the costs for teaching, advising, and research. The decline in the main sources of aid has created a very challenging environment for African universities today. There are shortages of books, journals, lab equipment and supplies, research resources, and salary payments. In the midst of this, there is unprecedented demand for higher education, making universities more crowded and stretching their resources even more thinly.

HIV/AIDS and other social and economic crises create new demands on universities but also reduce the resources available. University personnel are affected by HIV/AIDS, and funding is drawn away from higher education to address the crisis. Economic and political turmoil in some African countries has discouraged greater investment, disrupted school years, and led to the destruction of facilities and the loss of human resources.

However, new attention is being given to the revitalization of African universities. A report by the Task Force on Higher Education and Society, funded by the World Bank, called for new investment by lending agencies. The Partnership for Higher Education in Africa is an initiative of seven U.S.-based foundations supporting improvements in African universities. It focuses its activities in nine countries—Egypt, Ghana, Madagascar, Mozambique, Nigeria, South Africa, Tanzania, Uganda, and Kenya—with a total population of over 460 million people. Through 2010, the Partnership provided $440 million in grants for education, which directly and indirectly improved conditions for 4.1 million students at 379 universities and colleges.

SUMMARY

Education is an expensive enterprise, and failure to consider the costs and financing can cripple education efforts. However, experience in Africa has shown that education decision makers must balance attention to the economics of education with the political and pedagogical goals. Education must be about learning and serving the goals of society. In times of austerity, emphasis is placed on reducing spending, but the focus must return to the purpose and benefit of education on the continent.

PUSH FOR DEMOCRATIC PARTICIPATION IN EDUCATION

One outcome of globalization is global competitiveness in education, which pushes education decision makers to focus on economic performance, accountability, and quality. African governments are under enormous pressure to increase public spending on education and find other sources of income to fund the expansion of educational opportunities. The pressure to introduce market mechanisms into public school systems is strong in many African countries with insufficient public resources, declining quality, and policy agendas set increasingly by international financial institutions.

At the same time, Africa has experienced a wave of democratic change. Over the past 25 years, pressure has built at the local level for a greater voice for the people. In education this has translated into greater say in decisions affecting schools. The result has been tremendous experimentation with policy-making models and decentralization of school governance and financing.

A government worker speaks about education policy in a public forum, Sierra Leone. For many countries in Africa, democracy holds the promise of a better education system. Schools are extremely important, and the public wants to be involved in policy making that will affect schooling.

CONSULTATIVE EDUCATION POLICY-MAKING MODELS

Numerous African countries have departed from the top-down "behind closed doors" approach to education policy making to experiment with participatory policy-making models. In each of the four mechanisms discussed here—a national conference, a master plan, an education policy commission, and video-enhanced consultative conferences—it is the commitment to a truly consultative process that determines whether policy formation is enriched and support for new policies is built.

BENIN'S ETATS GÉNÉRAUX

In 1990 Benin emerged from a Marxist military regime, which went bankrupt. It was part of the first wave of African countries moving to democracy. The new government held a broad forum on education, known as the *Etats Généraux de l'Education* (General State of Education). Four hundred people attended, representing every government ministry, all offices of the National Education Ministry, trade associations, external funding agencies, non-governmental organizations (NGOs), students, and parents. The conference succeeded in sharing information and promoting dialogue. However, urban centers were overrepresented, and many participants focused on "lack of resources" as the top problem. The government made no commitment to act upon the demands of participants, and because the proceedings of the *Etats Généraux* were never circulated, little follow-up effort was made.

CREATING A MASTER PLAN IN MAURITIUS

Several factors prompted Mauritius in 1990 to take a radical look at its whole education system. The EFA Conference in Jomtein, a meeting reviewing technical education and training, the establishment of a new government, and increased demand for a more skilled labor force for a rapidly growing economy all gave impetus to a comprehensive review.

The preparation of Mauritius's education plan started in 1990, and by year's end a proposal was made by the high-level Steering Committee for its major element: moving to nine-year schooling for all children. Wide public consultations were held with teachers, school managers, principals, and students. The public was invited to submit comments and make suggestions. Over 200 measures were proposed. Seminars were held to discuss the status of teachers and other specific education issues. A draft master plan was published and discussed at a national seminar attended by a wide range of stakeholders: teachers, heads of schools, school managers, higher education administrators, PTAs (Parent-Teacher Associations), trade unions, NGOs, and others. The seminar deliberations led to a revision of the draft plan.

The consultative process was a search for consensus, which was viewed as a fundamental cultural value of Mauritian society. Consultation takes time, and the plan took more than twice as long to produce as had originally been anticipated. With a detailed master plan, Mauritius was able to take charge and negotiate successfully with foreign aid agencies. The country's Ministry of Education provided strong leadership, which enabled the government to take advantage of foreign expertise without allowing the aid agencies to dominate the process.

UGANDA'S REVIEW COMMISSION AND WHITE PAPER COMMITTEE

Uganda has a long history, dating from the colonial period, of appointing education review commissions every 10 years. The 1987–1989 Education Policy Review Commission was established one year after Yoweri Museveni came to power, ending a long guerrilla war. A new commitment was made to participatory democracy, liberalization of the economy, national unity, and accelerated development. The new government sought to gain legitimacy for its policies through citizen participation and deep consultation. The Education Policy Review Commission held public meetings and solicited 496 memoranda and resource papers. Commissioners traveled to towns throughout Uganda and conducted study tours in eight neighboring countries. Even so, many criticized the effort for focusing on input from the usual urban elites rather than community actors. The commission lacked the popular touch that Museveni's National Resistance Movement wanted. As a result, in December 1989 a white paper process was started to reopen and widen the debate on education policy issues.

Ordinarily, the writing of a white paper, a cabinet-level policy document, is a fairly quick exercise; Uganda's education white

Ugandan president Yoweri Museveni addresses the United Nations. At the start of his presidency, Museveni instituted an education review commission to research the will of the Ugandan people in regards to schooling policy. Ugandans discussed and debated policy until a consensus was reached. By working directly with the people, the Museveni government sought to legitimize its claim to power through democratic representation.

paper could have been expected to draw heavily from the Education Policy Review Commission report. However, the process resulted in a complete rewriting of the report. With strong support from the education minister and the president, a bottom-up, consensus-building process fed into the writing of the white paper. Policy proposals were widely discussed, senior Ministry of Education officials were consulted, and drafts were reviewed at the district level by political councils. Public debate was encouraged through radio and television programs. A consultative conference was held with representatives from various civil society organizations. Finally, an extended debate in Parliament was held in October 1994, ending the five-and-a-half-year consultative procedure. Many more citizens participated in the policy formation process than ever before. However, the lengthy procedure frustrated aid agencies, many of which set their priorities outside of the consultative practice.

BOTSWANA: USING VIDEO TO BRING MANY VOICES TO THE DISCUSSION

In 1988–1989, Botswana's Ministry of Education initiated a series of consultative conferences to support a dialogue between government and citizens regarding education issues. The ministry used videotape as a way to bring parents', pupils', and communities' voices to national leaders and allow rural communities to hear from the government. The aim was to develop common understandings of the education issues facing the country. The dialogues focused on four issues: the problem of school dropouts; the changed purpose of the curriculum; the role of community in developing and operating schools; and communication about education changes. For each issue a short video was made using interviews with a wide range of stakeholders. The first participative conference was held in the capital, Gaborone, and was directed at national leadership. The videos were shown to small groups of people who then heard from a panel of respondents and discussed the issue. Participants broke into working groups to consider various policy options and then reported back to the whole conference. Seeing fellow citizens express their ideas and emotions about an education issue reminded conference participants about the local reality and helped to keep the discussion grounded. An additional videotape was made at the conference capturing some of the discussions and responses of national leaders. Following the national conference, the videos were used in a similar way in three regional conferences. The series of "grassroots policy dialogues" helped to build a common perspective and rebuild public confidence in the policy-making process.

PUSH FOR DECENTRALIZATION

Since 1990 over 30 sub-Saharan African countries have implemented one or more major education decentralization initiatives. The interest in decentralization has arisen for several reasons. African governments observed the collapse of Eastern European socialism and, with it, the demise of central planning. The fiscal crisis of the 1980s and the accompanying Structural Adjustment Programs necessitated a search for more cost-effective alternatives. In addition, new political freedom in many parts of the continent put pressure on governments to share authority.

Most decentralization efforts have meant moving administrative responsibilities to local government offices or requiring lower levels of government, such as provinces, regions, or municipalities, to pay for some of the costs of providing education. In such cases the government might operate more efficiently, but quality will not necessarily improve.

Transferring authority down to school and community levels is usually supported for two reasons. First, it has the potential to improve the running of schools and, indirectly, student achievement. Second, it is believed that citizen participation in democratic processes will strengthen the transformation of society. Several African national experiments at the school and community level are worth examining.

THE SOUTH AFRICAN EXPERIENCE

The experience of South Africa is interesting because it has moved further than any other sub-Saharan African country in introducing a national model of school-based governance and financing. This model demands attention also because of South Africa's size and importance: a country of 44 million, with 12 million students, South Africa boasts one of the continent's most vibrant economies. Many Africans will be closely watching the South African experience with decentralized school financing and governance.

In the wake of the destructive impact of apartheid on authority structures and school-community relations, the South African government recognized the need for new structures and procedures to elicit and support local participation. South Africa was motivated to decentralize by political and economic considerations. Politically, the post-apartheid government was committed to extending democracy through citizen participation. It was further dedicated to redressing apartheid inequities, including improving the quality of education for those who were disadvantaged. Economically, the government found itself with insufficient financial resources to meet the educational needs of the country.

South African policy called for the establishment of school governing bodies (SGBs) composed of the principal and elected representatives of parents, teachers, non-teaching staff, and (in secondary schools) students. Parents would be in the majority and chair the body. A basic set of functions and powers would be assigned to all SGBs, including setting admissions policy, making recommendations for teaching and non-teaching appointments to the provincial government, managing school finances, setting school fees, and raising additional funds. SGBs could apply to have additional functions.

The policy was announced in 1996, and implementation started in 1998. Research to date has found that the goals of decentralization for improved equity, expanded democracy, and improved quality have not been met, except in resource-rich areas. Allowing schools to set fees, even at the primary level, has made the resource inequalities across schools worse. In some settings it has been a struggle to get parents to run for the SGB, partly because the work is voluntary and many parents are not

Students in South Africa's Athlone High School for Girls, located in suburban Johannesburg, play a board game called "The Magical AIDS Journey" to learn about HIV/AIDS. South Africa's educational decentralization policies have produced mixed results, benefiting schools in more affluent areas (such as Athlone) while failing to address the problems of poor rural schools.

able to spend the time required to fulfill the many legislative conditions placed on the operations of SGBs.

While parents serve as the majority on the school boards, their practical authority is often determined by the principal and school staff. School boards typically have not focused on improving the quality of schools. Rural schools serving poor communities (the majority in South Africa) can only charge low fees and thus have limited resources to use. Meanwhile, affluent urban schools, especially the former white schools, are able to raise large sums of money to improve physical facilities and hire extra teachers. To date, decentralization has not led to greater social equity in South Africa. A recent policy review is expected to lead to changes in school fee policies.

MALI'S ASSOCIATIONS DES PARENTS DES ELEVES

Associations des Parents des Eleves (Associations of Parents of Students), or APEs, were established in Mali by legislation in 1960, but many existed only on paper or were perceived as corrupt. Members were, in effect, elected for life and prone to patronage. Following Mali's multiparty elections in 1992, APEs were reconsidered as potentially powerful organizations for the improvement of schools, as well as mechanisms to reinvigorate public confidence and engagement in social services. APEs were reconstituted with new membership rules, governance regulations, and considerable training provided by an international NGO and supported by aid funding. APEs now raise funds for scholarships, monitor quality, support staffing and professional development, educate parents about issues, mediate conflicts between parents and teachers, and advocate with the government. An individual APE in a village is part of a larger federation that reaches up to district, regional, and national levels, interacting with the Ministry of Education at each level.

Some APEs proved so effective that they were asked to take on development projects outside of education, such as rebuilding a health center. In some villages, community members agreed to pay taxes with the condition that the funds be used for school maintenance.

NAMIBIA'S COMMUNITY AND SCHOOL EFFORTS

When Namibia gained its independence in 1990, the top educational priority was to dismantle the apartheid education system and replace it with democratic practice. At the community level this meant strengthening the relationship between communities and local schools and ensuring that communities helped to define the future of education. Several mechanisms were used to promote community participation in educational decision making, including school boards, a code of conduct, and student representative councils. As the country's education minister said, "In the final analysis the type of education which will emerge in post-colonial Namibia will very much depend upon the type of partnership which will develop between the new government and the people."

In 1990 the Ministry of Education and Culture requested that communities elect representatives to school boards and contribute to the construction of new classrooms as partners in educational development. The Namibian Educational Code of Conduct for Schools was written with assistance from the student union, NANSO. This document lays out the rights and responsibilities of students, teachers, principals, and school boards. It discusses the democratic processes needed in the administration of schools, including the establishment of school boards with parent, teacher, and student representation. The writing of this code amounted to a redefinition of the relationships between learners, parents, and teachers. Specifically, the code states that principals and school boards have the responsibility to initiate and support parent participation in school affairs, and teachers have the responsibility to consult with students' parents. These are significant departures from the role of school committees under the apartheid regime.

A third mechanism for democratic decision making is the student representative council (SRC), a form of student government. Since independence, SRCs have been giving students experience with democratic structures and practices, particularly at the secondary school level.

SUMMARY

As a result of experiments with devolving control of schools to local levels, it is slowly being recognized that decentralization does not necessarily lead to democratization. But the potential can be nurtured. There are now numerous examples in Africa of efforts to promote popular participation. Knowledge and respect for community perspectives are keys to success. It is important not to assume that communities are able and willing to take on greater financial and governance responsibilities for schooling. Parents' time and effort is a scarce resource, and participation needs to be nurtured and supported. Legislation alone is not sufficient.

PERSISTING INEQUALITIES

No picture of education in Africa would be complete without an examination of educational inequalities that exist at three levels: between Africa and other regions of the world (an issue that has already been treated in depth in Chapter 2); between individual countries or clusters of African countries; and within individual African countries. Each level suggests different approaches to support change.

INEQUALITIES BETWEEN AFRICAN COUNTRIES

Colonial legacies have left a lasting impression on patterns of education participation. Countries that were formerly British colonies, plus Namibia and Liberia, are referred to as Anglophone (English-speaking) countries, even though they may have multiple national languages. The 22 former French colonies are classified as Francophone. And the former Portuguese colonies of Mozambique, Angola,

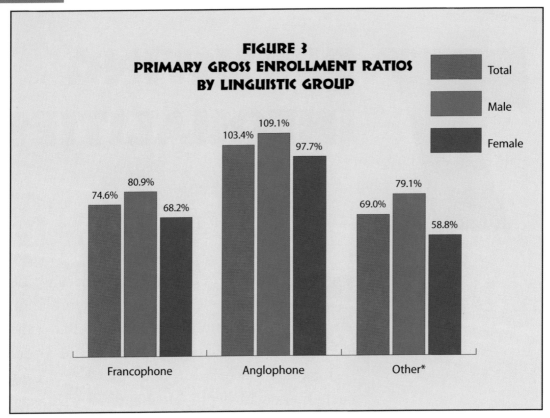

FIGURE 3
PRIMARY GROSS ENROLLMENT RATIOS BY LINGUISTIC GROUP

* Includes the five Lusophone countries of Angola, Cape Verde, Equatorial Guinea, Guinea-Bissau, and Mozambique, as well as Ethiopia and Somalia.
Source: UIS Database.

Guinea-Bissau, Equatorial Guinea, Cape Verde, and São Tomé and Príncipe are referred to as Lusophone countries.

Anglophone countries have higher enrollment ratios—at all levels of education—than Francophone or Lusophone countries. Overall, the primary gross enrollment ratio in Anglophone countries exceeds 100 percent, with nearly 98 percent female access. In Francophone countries, by contrast, GER averages only about 75 percent, with a significant gender gap (almost 13 percent). According to UNESCO, five Lusophone countries, along with Ethiopia and Somalia, have a 79 percent enrollment ratio for males, but a ratio of only about 59 percent for females.

The colonial legacy can also be seen in patterns of education participation at the secondary level. Enrollment ratios average

37 percent for Anglophone countries but only 20 percent for Francophone countries, with a 9.6 percent gender gap. The Lusophone countries plus Ethiopia and Somalia also have low enrollment rates, averaging 19 percent, with an 8.6 percent gender gap.

Female representation in the teaching force varies significantly across linguistic groups. Females make up approximately half of the primary teachers in Anglophone countries, but in the eight Francophone countries for which data is available, 25 percent or fewer of the primary teachers are female. In the Lusophone country of Mozambique, only 28 percent of primary teachers are female. Low literacy rates among women dramatically reduce the pool of potential female teachers.

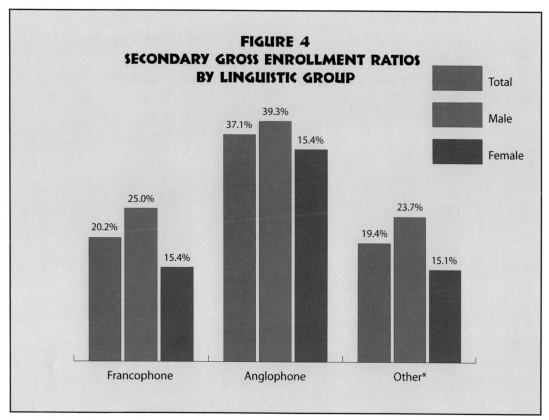

FIGURE 4
SECONDARY GROSS ENROLLMENT RATIOS BY LINGUISTIC GROUP

* Includes the five Lusophone countries of Angola, Cape Verde, Equatorial Guinea, Guinea-Bissau, and Mozambique, as well as Ethiopia and Somalia.
Source: UIS Database.

Francophone countries have a female literacy rate of 41 percent, compared with a rate of 62 percent for males. An even larger gender gap exists in Lusophone countries, where female literacy is 40 percent and male literacy 71 percent.

Geography also plays a role, as evidenced by the very low enrollment rates in the countries bordering the Sahel, the semi-arid region of north-central Africa that lies south of the Sahara Desert. The Sahelian countries, which are among the poorest on the continent, also have the lowest rates of primary school participation; primary GER averages 59 percent, and there is a 17 percent gender gap. For secondary school, GER in the Sahelian countries is 21 percent, but the gender gap is smaller, at only 9 percent. Figure 6 compares the adult literacy rates for the four Sahelian countries of Burkina Faso, Chad, Mali, and Niger (no

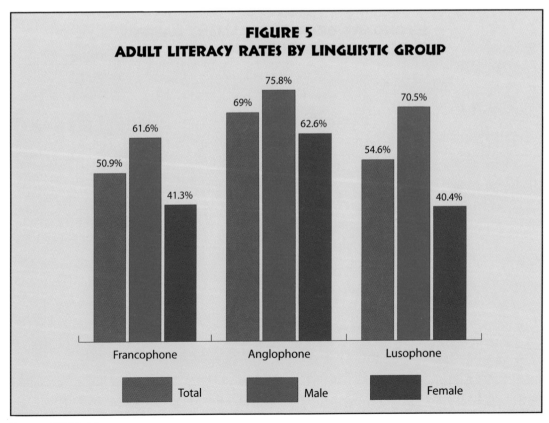

Source: UIS Database.

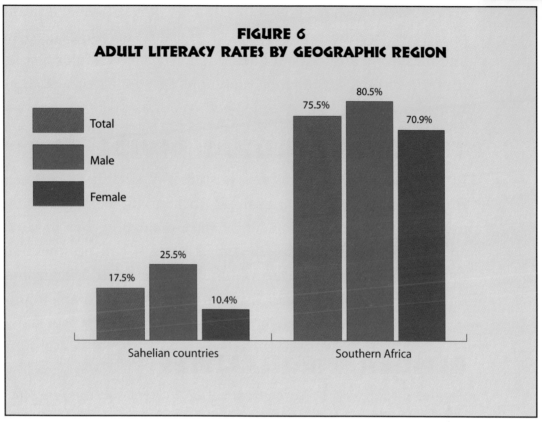

FIGURE 6
ADULT LITERACY RATES BY GEOGRAPHIC REGION

Source: UIS Database.

data is available for Mauritania) with those of the southern African countries of Botswana, South Africa, Namibia, Swaziland, Zimbabwe, Lesotho, and Mozambique. Overall adult literacy rates are only 18 percent for the Sahelian countries, compared with 76 percent in southern Africa. Female literacy rates vary even more, at 10 percent in the Sahelian countries and 71 percent in southern Africa.

EDUCATIONAL INEQUALITIES WITHIN COUNTRIES

Although African countries made tremendous progress in addressing racial inequalities inherited from pre-independence times, educational opportunities in Africa remain unequally distributed. Major disparities exist within countries across lines of gender, wealth, geography, and ethnicity. There are significant differences in education rates between males and females, urban and rural populations, poor and affluent segments. Major disparities can also be seen among marginalized populations, such as nomadic peoples.

THE URBAN-RURAL DIVIDE

In some countries, the main educational inequality is between rural and urban areas. For example, in Benin 37 percent of children in urban areas complete primary education, but in rural areas only 26 percent do. A similar pattern can be found in Mozambique, Burkina Faso, Guinea, Madagascar, Niger, and Togo. The percentage of girls in rural areas who complete primary school is even lower.

GENDER INEQUALITIES

Gender disparities in African education systems become increasingly pronounced as one goes up the education pyramid. While about 45 percent of the primary school students are female, women make up less than one-third of the university-level students in sub-Saharan Africa. Yet considerable progress has been made since the independence period. In 1960, females made up 34 percent of the primary students, 25 percent of the secondary students, and only 10 percent of the university students. Between the 1989–1990 and 2002–2003 school years, all sub-Saharan countries except Ghana, Eritrea, and São Tomé and Príncipe improved their primary

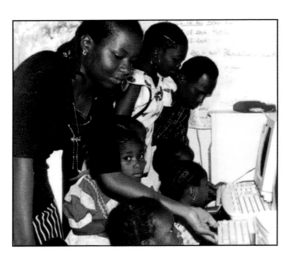

Aissata Ba received a scholarship from USAID in order to attend university, making her one of the few women in Senegal to get a higher education. Here she helps kids learn to use a computer.

enrollment gender gap. However, 12 countries still have a gender gap equal to 10 percent or more. Chad has the largest at 24 percent.

In the majority of African countries, females are underrepresented in the education system. There are exceptions, however.

TABLE 12
COUNTRIES WITH HIGHEST AND LOWEST GENDER GAP IN PRIMARY NET ENROLLMENT RATIOS, 2002–2003

COUNTRY	GENDER GAP MALE NER–FEMALE NER
Chad	24%
Swaziland	16%
Guinea	15%
Niger	14%
Nigeria	14%
Côte d'Ivoire	13%
Equatorial Guinea	13%
Ghana	12%
Mali	11%
Burkina Faso	11%
Burundi	10%
Ethiopia	10%
Kenya	0% (parity)
South Africa	0% (parity)
Swaziland	0% (parity)
Madagascar	+1%
Zimbabwe	+1%
Mauritius	+2%
Rwanda	+3%
Botswana	+4%
Namibia	+5%
Lesotho	+6%

Source: UNESCO Global Education Report 2005, Tables 3 and 5.

As the bottom of Table 12 indicates, seven African countries had higher proportions of females than males enrolled in primary school in 2002–2003, and three other countries reported gender parity.

At the secondary level in 2002–2003, five sub-Saharan African countries (Botswana, Cape Verde, Lesotho, Namibia, and South Africa) had higher proportions of females than males, while two more (Mauritius and Seychelles) reported gender parity. It is interesting that four of these countries are located in southern Africa and all but Lesotho are middle-income countries. Lesotho is evidence that poverty is not the only factor explaining low female participation rates.

In the area of adult literacy, the gender gap in Africa persists. In 1990 about 4 in 10 females (39.5 percent) were literate, compared with about 6 in 10 males (59.3 percent). A decade later, female literacy had risen to 52.5 percent, but male literacy was still considerably higher, at 68.8 percent. But these aggregate figures mask the extreme disparity within certain countries. In seven countries—Angola, Central African Republic, Democratic Republic of the Congo, Liberia, Chad, Togo, and Mozambique—the gender gap in adult literacy rates exceeds 25 percent. One of the reasons for the lack of progress may be that all of these countries were the sites of recent armed conflict.

A considerable body of knowledge now exists regarding the barriers to girls' participation in schooling. These barriers include cost, quality of facilities, school quality, and social norms and expectations.

The costs of schooling prevent many poor children in Africa from receiving an education. Some parents cannot afford to send any of their children to school; others must choose one child over another to receive an education. The direct costs of schooling, while perhaps modest by Western standards, can be a major impediment in impoverished Africa. These costs include tuition, fees, uniforms, supplies, and transportation. But indirect costs—the loss of a child's labor or income while the child attends school—may also make education unaffordable for the poorest. The labor of girls in the household (cooking, cleaning, preparing food, watching younger siblings) is often critical as it allows other members of the household to work.

Schools with poor physical facilities—for example, those that lack running water and toilets—have been found to deter attendance by girls. Many parents in Africa are unwilling to send their daughters to schools that have no accommodations for hygiene. Distance, too, is a factor; many African parents consider it unsafe for girls to travel a long way from their home.

This young girl in Zambia collects water for her family before school. The daily task of getting water for the household keeps many African girls from attending school entirely, as the nearest source of safe water may be several miles distant from rural villages.

Poor school quality may also deter parents from sending their girls to school. "Quality" is a very broad term, but it includes the perceptions of parents and children as well as objective measures, such as student achievement or teacher qualifications. Important indicators of good school quality may include freedom from sexual harassment, regular teacher attendance, the absence of abusive disciplinary practices, the availability of teaching and learning resources, relevant curriculum, and evidence that children are learning.

Social norms and expectations—which are set by families, communities, schools, the labor market, and society at large—constitute the fourth set of factors that often stand in the way of African girls' school attendance. They include work options deemed acceptable, work opportunities, expected age of marriage, school subjects considered appropriate, and behavioral norms. All of these influence parents' decisions to send girls to school and support their staying to complete the schooling cycle.

Considerable international attention is currently focused on attaining equal access for boys and girls, but the gender inequalities in Africa go beyond access. There are differences in attainment and achievement, which may be due to bias in curriculum, teaching and learning materials, and school and classroom practices. In recent years, greater attention has been given to how schooling is experienced differently by boys and girls. School textbooks and curricula can both mirror society, with all its inequalities, and promote the ideals of an equitable society.

AFRICAN ORGANIZATIONS ADDRESSING GENDER INEQUALITY

An integrated approach to addressing gender inequalities has been found to work best. This means addressing the range of barriers. Reducing direct and indirect costs, improving school quality, and addressing social impediments require simultaneous attention.

Numerous African organizations work to address gender inequalities in education. The following are highlights:

The Forum for African Women Educationalists (FAWE) is an organization that seeks to ensure that girls have the opportunity to attend school, complete their studies, and perform well at all levels. Founded in 1992 by five female ministers of education, it now includes more than 40 African female cabinet ministers and other high-level educators. FAWE is a pan-African non-governmental organization with a secretariat in Nairobi and a network of 33 national chapters. FAWE works with partners to create positive societal attitudes and practices that promote equity for girls in educational access, retention, performance, and quality. The group funds demonstration projects and advocacy work.

Female Education in Mathematics and Science in Africa (FEMSA) is a project of the Association for the Development of Education in Africa (ADEA) Working Group on Female Participation, hosted by FAWE. It aims to improve the participation and performance of girls in science, mathematics, and technical subjects at the primary and secondary school levels.

The Alliance for Community Action on Female Education (the Alliance) was created to channel funding and other types of assistance to non-governmental organizations promoting female access to education. The Alliance seeks to ensure a healthy partnership between governments and NGOs in creating multiple channels for educational opportunity. It has facilitated networking among local NGOs and community-based organizations and provided technical support through the provision of small grants.

The Partnership for Strategic Resource Planning in Africa (SRP) aims to build capacity in participating countries to carry out research aimed at advancing the girls' education agenda. It also

Laura Bush, the U.S. first lady, and her daughter Jenna meet in Rwanda with members of the Forum for African Women Educationalists, 2005. The organization supports initiatives to ensure that girls have equal access to education.

works to identify how national education resources might be better used to increase gender equity in educational opportunities. Nine countries are participating in the SRP initiative: Ethiopia, Ghana, Guinea, Malawi, Mali, Senegal, Tanzania, Uganda, and Zambia.

SUMMARY

The education MDGs and the Education for All movement aim to ensure that all children have the opportunity for education, regardless of gender, wealth, ethnicity, geographic location, political circumstances, or learning needs. Educational inequalities

MILLENNIUM DEVELOPMENT GOALS PERTAINING TO EDUCATION

MDG 2: Achieve universal primary education

Target: Ensure that, by 2015, children everywhere, boys and girls alike, will be able to complete a full course of primary schooling.

Indicators:
Primary NER (net enrollment ratio)
% children reaching grade 5
Youth literacy rate

MDG 3: Promote gender equality & empower women

Target: Eliminate gender disparity in primary and secondary education, preferably by 2005 and in all levels of education no later than 2015.

Indicators:
Ratio of girls to boys in primary, secondary, & tertiary education
Ratio of literate females to males
Female share of non-agricultural wage employment
% seats in parliament held by women

must be addressed by more than educational change. Educational inequalities are influenced by poverty, historical practice, current habits, legal systems, and discriminatory practices. Therefore, change requires both an awareness of the nature of the inequalities and the political will to address them inside and outside of education. A political commitment from senior levels of governments can make change possible. But there is also a need for partnerships between public and private groups for the sharing of ideas and rededication to meeting continuing challenges.

8 NEW CHALLENGES

Progress in advancing educational opportunities in Africa faces the growing threat of the HIV/AIDS epidemic, as well as armed conflict and its aftermath. The toll of both threats is felt by individuals, including children, as well as by education systems. In both cases women are particularly vulnerable.

HIV/AIDS AND EDUCATION

There are now 15 million children under age 18 who have been orphaned by HIV/AIDS, according to UNICEF, and 80 percent of them are in sub-Saharan Africa. By 2010 it is estimated that 18 million children in sub-Saharan Africa will have lost one or both parents to the disease. Thirteen sub-Saharan African countries currently have more than 250,000 HIV/AIDS orphans, and together these countries are home to over 10 million orphans.

In addition to the orphans, 1.9 million children under 14 years of age are themselves living

(Opposite) The Cwalinkungu Junior Secondary School in South Africa gives children orphaned by AIDS a chance to get an education. In 2003 South Africa had 1.1 million AIDS orphans. With no parents to pay school fees and with survival a constant struggle, many orphans cannot afford to attend school.

with HIV. Sub-Saharan Africa has 70 percent (25 million in 2003) of the adults and children living with HIV/AIDS.

HIV/AIDS is more than a disease. It is a development disaster, hampering efforts to improve the welfare of African peoples and reversing the gains made over the last four decades in improving social, economic, and cultural conditions.

THE IMPACT OF HIV/AIDS ON EDUCATION SYSTEMS

HIV/AIDS is putting an enormous strain on African education systems, and many ministries of education have been unable to respond effectively. The epidemic is decreasing the size of the teaching force. UNESCO estimates that HIV/AIDS will claim the lives of 10 percent of the teachers in Africa by 2008. In the KwaZulu-Natal Province of South Africa it is estimated that 68,000 educators will be lost by 2010. Teacher education institutions, whose staffs also are affected by the disease, cannot train the next generation of teachers fast enough. Large numbers of education administrators will also be lost.

TABLE 13
AFRICAN COUNTRIES WITH MORE THAN 250,000
HIV/AIDS ORPHANS, 2003

COUNTRY	NUMBER OF HIV/AIDS ORPHANS (0–17 YEARS)
Nigeria	1,800,000
South Africa	1,100,000
Tanzania	980,000
Zimbabwe	980,000
Uganda	940,000
Democratic Republic of Congo	770,000
Ethiopia	720,000
Kenya	650,000
Zambia	630,000
Malawi	500,000
Mozambique	470,000
Côte d'Ivoire	310,000
Burkina Faso	260,000

Source: UNICEF 2005.

At the school level, the disease places an increased burden on school operations. Teachers who are infected with HIV, or who have HIV-positive family members, experience decreased productivity because of chronic health issues and increased caregiving responsibilities. Likewise, children affected by HIV/AIDS become habitually absent. In Swaziland, net enrollment dropped from 93 percent to 80 percent between 1983 and 1996, due in part to HIV/AIDS. The increased orphan population presents growing demands on schools, which are not equipped to deal with the special psychosocial and economic needs of orphans and child-headed households. Communities overstretched by the epidemic are less able to participate in school affairs. It is anticipated that HIV/AIDS will further reduce the length of time children stay in school as well as their achievement.

The burden of HIV/AIDS falls disproportionately on girls, whether or not they are infected. When households are affected by HIV/AIDS, the demand for girls' labor increases. Girls are forced to become caregivers for sick parents or younger siblings.

A concerted but inadequate effort is under way, supported by governments, community groups, and international organizations, to help children and families touched by HIV/AIDS. A multi-sector approach is necessary, since the epidemic involves health, education, industry, and economic development and it touches individuals, households, communities, and institutions. Already strained budgets make scaling up HIV/AIDS services difficult, and governments face tough decisions on where to cut back in order to free up resources to address the impact of HIV/AIDS on education systems.

When parents are incapacitated by AIDS, young girls, like the one pictured here from Mozambique, often take over the responsibilities of running the family and caring for smaller children.

USING EDUCATION TO FIGHT HIV/AIDS

The highest priority is to stop the spread of the disease. Education, both formal and informal, plays a role in this effort. Education has been described as the "social vaccine." It works by exposing students to warnings about HIV/AIDS and messages about delaying sexual activity. In 1990 HIV prevalence rates in Uganda were similar for all people aged 18–29, regardless of their education. By 1995, however, after the introduction of HIV/AIDS education in school and public campaigns, differences began to appear. By 2001 the HIV prevalence rate had dropped to approximately 2 percent among persons in the 18–29 age group with secondary education, and to 6 to 7 percent among those with primary education. Meanwhile, those with no schooling had a 12 percent prevalence rate.

In many contexts, combating the spread of HIV/AIDS is being integrated into a broader effort to promote and protect educational quality. There are many promising efforts in the use of education to prevent HIV/AIDS, including peer education, the incorporation of sexual and reproductive health education and life skills training into the curriculum, and the preparation of teachers and principals. But the effectiveness of some of these efforts is not known, and many programs are on a small scale.

EDUCATION ISSUES FOR CONFLICT AND POST-CONFLICT SITUATIONS

The Education for All agenda includes a commitment to children affected by conflict, national calamity, and instability. In recent years Africa has suffered from numerous armed conflicts, with protracted violence occurring in Mozambique, Sierra Leone, Angola, Somalia, northern Uganda, western Sudan, Rwanda, Burundi, Liberia, Democratic Republic of the Congo, Congo, and Chad. For children—including child soldiers and noncombatant victims of violence—these conflicts have created special needs that regular school systems may not serve very well.

CHILD SOLDIERS

The Convention on the Rights of the Child specifies 15 years as the minimum age at which someone may serve as a soldier. Across Africa, however, even younger children have been recruited or forced to fight in various conflicts.

Child soldiers need to be reintegrated back into society and helped to build productive lives. Education plays an important

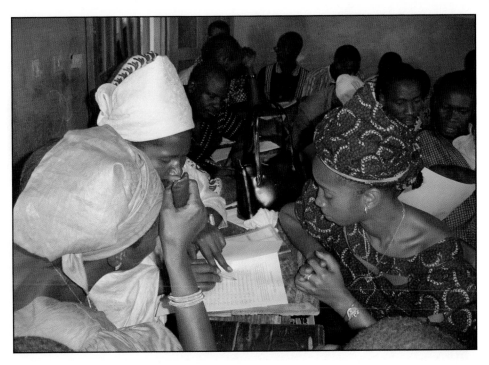

Teachers in Guinea review materials for their HIV/AIDS awareness training. By incorporating AIDS education into the curriculum, African countries hope to teach younger generations how to protect themselves from infection.

role in this difficult effort. But most often child soldiers cannot enroll in regular schools or pick up where they left off before their recruitment or abduction. The reason is not primarily that these children, many of whom have spent years in the field, may be considerably older than other children at the same educational level. It is, rather, that they have witnessed and participated in extreme violence, causing profound psychological and emotional issues. In addition, many communities are reluctant to accept hardened fighters back into their midst.

Girls are not recognized as child soldiers and, therefore, have been largely ignored in post-conflict reintegration efforts under the belief that they were "wives" or forced laborers but not "real fighters." Research is revealing, however, that girls play a diverse set of roles in African conflicts; they may be active soldiers, spies, porters, medics, or slave laborers. Their experiences are

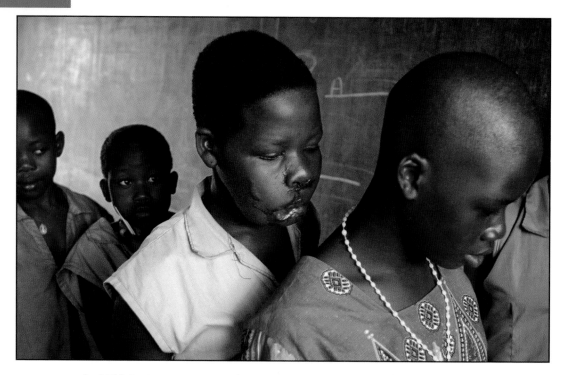

In 2002 Apoko Evelyn was abducted by the Lord's Resistance Army in Uganda. She was injured by a grenade when the rebel group was attacked by the Ugandan army, and her wound was left to heal untreated. She eventually escaped to a rehabilitation center in Lira, Uganda.

often very different from those of boys. Since the mid-1990s, girls have been kidnapped and forced into wartime service in Angola, Burundi, Liberia, Mozambique, Rwanda, Sierra Leone, and Uganda. Sometimes girls "choose" to become soldiers, although this is often to avoid being physically and sexually abused or to gain access to the only food in the area. After the conflict ends, they face a greater stigma if they were raped and gave birth to children of their captors. Yet female combatants desire access to education and skills training to help them rebuild their lives and become productive adults.

Reintegration efforts often provide help in tracing families separated by conflict. They also provide support to families caring for former child soldiers. Ex-combatants are enrolled in appropriate educational courses (basic education or vocational training) and youth programs such as apprenticeships, small businesses, and sports activities.

NONCOMBATANT CHILDREN AFFECTED BY CONFLICT

Far larger numbers of children in Africa are not participants in the fighting but still have their lives—including their education—disrupted by armed conflict. They may become internally displaced persons or international refugees. They may live in or outside refugee camps. In recent years, international support for providing education in emergency situations has grown. The Inter-Agency Network for Education in Emergencies (INEE) has established

Children at a village school in the Darfur region of Sudan, which has been torn by fighting over the past decade. In many African countries beset by conflict, children have borne an especially harsh burden, creating unique problems that education systems have struggled to address.

standards for the provision of education in emergency situations. Both UNESCO and UNHCR (the United Nations refugee agency) work with a wide range of relief organizations to provide education in conflict and post-conflict settings. In each setting, the question arises as to whether children would be best served in camps, in host country government schools, or in new schools established for refugees outside of camps. Issues of language, curriculum, and likely time before repatriation are all considered. One of the newer initiatives is to use peace education curricula in camps to prevent continued cycles of conflict.

THE FUTURE OF EDUCATION IN AFRICA

Education in Africa has evolved through history, from its roots in indigenous educational practices through the influence of Islam and Christianity and the various colonial regimes. Each of these factors has left a legacy that varies across countries. This rich history of education on the continent is also marked by significant progress in reducing inequalities in educational opportunities and, in turn, social inequalities. An understanding of the nature of persisting inequalities provides a focus for future action.

Across the continent, experimentation with more participatory decision making is taking place. As with all experiments, some of the efforts will make lasting contributions and some will be short lived. Nonetheless, the trend toward broader engagement of civil society in decisions surrounding education is undeniable.

Many of the gains in expanding educational opportunity in Africa are gravely threatened by three burdens: crippling debt, HIV/AIDS, and

Public school students outside their school in Kenya. Africa's prospects in the 21st century hinge largely on how its countries meet the challenges of education.

the need to provide education in conflict and post-conflict situations. It is these threats that will be the greatest forces defining the future of education in Africa. The financial constraints faced by many African countries are severely limiting further expansion of educational opportunity and improvement of quality. The situation argues for an exploration of alternative forms for educating teachers and students, including sound applications of information and communications technologies. Standard models for education are proving too slow and ineffective in urgently addressing the HIV/AIDS crisis and identifying ways to meet the complex demands of conflict and post-conflict situations. New thinking is required because the future of Africa rests, to a large extent, with how the next generation is educated.

Glossary

ANGLOPHONE AFRICA—the former British colonies south of the Sahara Desert, plus Ethiopia and Liberia, which speak English as a national language.

DEVELOPMENT BUDGET—a plan to finance long-term outlays such as physical infrastructure; also called "capital budget."

ETATS GÉNÉREAUX—a consultative conference on the "General State of Education;" a forum unique to Francophone Africa.

FRANCOPHONE AFRICA—the former French colonies south of the Sahara Desert.

GENDER GAP—the difference between the enrollment ratios of boys and the enrollment ratios of girls.

GENDER PARITY INDEX (GPI)—ratio of the female to male values of a given indicator. A GPI of 1 indicates parity between sexes.

GROSS ENROLLMENT RATIO (GER)—the number of students enrolled in a level of education, regardless of age, as a percentage of the population of official school age for that level. The gross enrollment ratio can be greater than 100 percent as a result of grade repetition and school entry at ages younger or older than the official age for that grade level.

LITERACY RATE, ADULT—the percentage of people age 15 and above who can, with understanding, both read and write a short, simple statement related to their everyday life.

LITERACY RATE, YOUTH—the percentage of people age 15–24 who can, with understanding, both read and write a short, simple statement related to their everyday life.

LUSOPHONE AFRICA—the former Portuguese colonies of Mozambique, Angola, Guinea-Bissau, São Tomé and Príncipe, and Cape Verde.

NET ENROLLMENT RATIO (NER)—the number of students enrolled in a level of education who are of official school age for that level, as a percentage of the population of official school age for that level. The net enrollment ratio cannot be greater than 100 percent.

RECURRENT EXPENDITURE ON EDUCATION—expenditure for goods and services consumed within the current year (and renewed if needed in the following year). It includes expenditure on staff salaries, pensions, and benefits; contracted or purchased services; other resources, including books and teaching materials; welfare services; and other current expenditure such as subsidies to students and households, furniture and minor equipment, minor repairs, fuel, telecommunications, travel, insurance, and rent.

STRUCTURAL ADJUSTMENT PROGRAMS (SAPS)—economic policies that countries had to follow in order to qualify for new World Bank and International Monetary Fund (IMF) loans to help them make debt repayments on the older debts owed to commercial banks, governments, and the World Bank. SAPs (replaced in the late 1990s by Poverty Reduction Strategy Papers or PRSPs) were designed for individual countries but had common guiding principles and features, including export-led growth; privatization and liberalization; and the inherent efficiency of the free market. SAPs generally required countries to devalue their currencies against the dollar; lift import and export restrictions; balance their budgets and not overspend; and remove price controls and state subsidies. Reductions in expenditures in education and health often occurred under SAPs.

UJAMAA—Swahili word meaning "family." Julius Nyerere and the Tanzanian government used the term to define the African roots of the socialist path Tanzania pursued.

Further Reading

Binns, Tony, Alan Dixon, and Etienne Nel. *Africa: Diversity and Development*. New York: Routledge, 2012.

Global Education Digest 2012: Opportunities Lost, The Impact of Grade Repetition and Early School Leaving. Montreal: UNESCO Institute for Statistics, 2012.

Mingat, Alain, and Kirsten Majgaard. *Education in Sub-Saharan Africa*. New York: World Bank, 2012.

Moulton, Jeanne, et al. *Education Reforms in Sub-Saharan Africa. Paradigm Lost?* Westport, Conn.: Greenwood Press, 2002.

Rotberg, Robert I. *Transformative Political Leadership: Making a Difference in the Developing World*. Chicago: University of Chicago Press, 2012.

Teferra, Damtew, and Philip G. Altbach, eds. *African Higher Education: An International Reference Handbook*. Bloomington: Indiana University Press, 2003.

UNICEF. *State of the World's Children 2012: Children in an Urban World*. New York: UNICEF, 2013.

Internet Resources

HTTP://WWW.ADEANET.ORG

The Association for the Development of Education in Africa (ADEA) is a partnership of African ministers of education and foreign assistance agencies providing financial and technical support to education. Technical working groups explore specific issues.

HTTP://WWW.FAWE.ORG

The Forum for African Women Educationalists (FAWE) promotes female participation in Africa. The site includes links to national FAWE offices and describes FAWE activities across the continent.

HTTP://WWW.INEESITE.ORG

The Inter-Agency Network for Education in Emergencies has a wide range of Good Practice Guides for education in emergencies and other current research and information. It serves as a resource for education practitioners around the world working in situations of emergencies and crisis.

HTTP://WWW.BC.EDU/RESEARCH/CIHE.HTML

The International Network for Higher Education in Africa site contains country profiles for higher education.

HTTP://WWW.UNMILLENNIUMPROJECT.ORG

The Millennium Project is an independent advisory body commissioned by the UN Secretary-General to advise on strategies for achieving the Millennium Development Goals. A series of Task Force reports are available on the site.

HTTP://WWW.FOUNDATION-PARTNERSHIP.ORG

The Partnership for Higher Education in Africa is an initiative of six U.S.-based foundations: the Carnegie Corporation of New York, the Ford Foundation, the John D. and Catherine T. MacArthur Foundation, the Rockefeller Foundation, the William and Flora Hewlett Foundation, and the Andrew W. Mellon Foundation.

HTTP://WWW.UNESCO.ORG/EDUCATION/EFA

The UNESCO Education for All site contains links to country reports and global monitoring of efforts to help all countries reach Education for All goals.

HTTP://WWW.UIS.UNESCO.ORG

The UNESCO Institute for Statistics provides a wide range of education data and analyses.

HTTP://WWW.NYEREREFOUNDATION.ORG

This page of the Mwalimu Nyerere Foundation site contains audio clips of Julius Nyerere.

Bibliography

Angula, Nahas (1990). "The National Integrated Education System for Emergent Namibia—Draft Proposal for Education Reform and Renewal." Secretary for Education and Culture, SWAPO of Namibia, Lusaka.

Angula, Nahas, and Suzanne Grant Lewis (1997). "Promoting Democratic Processes in Educational Decision Making: Reflections from Namibia's First 5 Years." *International Journal of Education Development* 17 (3): 233–249.

Association for the Development of African Education (1996). *Formulating Education Policy: Lessons and Experience from Sub-Saharan Africa*. Paris: DAE.

Bloch, Marianne; Josephine A. Beoku-Betts; and B. Robert Tabachnick (1998). *Women and Education in Sub-Saharan Africa*, edited by Marianne Bloch. Boulder, Colo.: Lynne Rienner.

Colclough, Christopher, et al. (2003). *Achieving Schooling for All in Africa: Costs, Commitment and Gender*. Burlington, Vt.: Ashgate Publishing Company.

Evans, David, ed. (1994). *Education Policy Formation in Africa: A Comparative Study of Five Countries*. Washington, D.C.: USAID.

Fafunwa, A. Babs, and J. U. Asiku, eds. (1982). *Education in Africa: A Comparative Survey*. London: George Allen & Unwin Publishers.

Herz, Barbara, and Gene B. Sperling (2004). *What Works in Girls' Education: Evidence and Policies from the Developing World*. Washington, D.C.: Council on Foreign Relations.

Inter-Agency Commission (UNDP, UNESCO, UNICEF, and World Bank) (1990). *Meeting basic learning needs: A vision for the 1990s*. Background document. World Conference on Education for All, March 5–9, Jomtein.

Kendall, Nancy O'Gara (2004). "Global Policy in Practice: The 'Successful Failure' of Free Primary Education in Malawi." Unpublished Ph.D. dissertation, Stanford University.

Lulat, Y.G.-M. (2003). "The Development of Higher Education in Africa: A Historical Survey." In *African Higher Education: An International Reference Handbook*, edited by Damtew Teferra and Philip G. Altbach, 15–31. Bloomington: Indiana University Press.

Marlow-Ferguson, Rebecca, ed. (2002). *World Education Encyclopedia*. New York: Gale Group.

Mazurana, Dyan (2004). "Reintegrating Girls from Fighting Forces in Africa." *id21 Insights Education.*

McPherson, Malcolm (2003). "Human Capital, Education, and Economic Growth: The Impacts of

HIV/AIDS." Center for Business and Government, Harvard University.

Moulton, Jeanne, et al. (2002). *Education Reforms in Sub-Saharan Africa: Paradigm Lost?* Westport, Conn: Greenwood Press.

Noble, J. (1977). "Education in Namibia." Unpublished MA Thesis, University of Nairobi, Faculty of Education.

Nyerere, Julius (1968). "Education for Self-Reliance." In Julius Nyerere, *Ujamaa—Essays on Socialism*, 44–75. Dar es Salaam: Government Printer.

Nyerere, Julius (1985). "Education in Tanzania." *Harvard Education Review* 55 (February): 45–52.

Okedara, J. T. (1994). "Africa, Anglophone: Adult Education." In *The International Encyclopedia of Education*, 2nd ed., edited by Torsten Husen and T. Neville Postlethwaite, 210–215. New York: Pergamon.

Oxfam. (1998). "Making Debt Relief Work: A Test of Political Will." Download at http://www.oxfam.org.uk/what_we_do/issues/debt_aid/debt_polwill.htm

Paasche, Karin I. "Mozambique." In *World Education Encyclopedia*, edited by Rebecca Marlow-Ferguson, 916–925. New York: Gale Group.

Samoff, Joel (1990). "'Modernizing' a Socialist Vision: Education in Tanzania." In *Education and Social Transition in the Third World*, edited by Martin

Carnoy and Joel Samoff, 209–273. Princeton, N.J.: Princeton University Press.

Samoff, Joel (2003). "No Teacher Guide, No Textbooks, No Chairs: Contending with Crisis in African Education." In *Comparative Education: The Dialectic of the Global and the Local*, edited by Robert F. Arnove and Carlos Alberto Torres, 409–445. New York: Rowman & Littlefield.

Samoff, Joel, and Suleman Sumra (1994). "From Planning to Marketing: Making Education and Training Policy in Tanzania." In *Coping with Crisis: Austerity, Adjustment and Human Resources*, edited by Joel Samoff, 134–172. New York: Cassell.

Task Force on Higher Education and Society (2000). *Higher Education in Developing Countries: Peril and Promise*. Washington, D.C.: World Bank.

Teferra, Damtew, and Philip G. Altbach (2003). "Trends and Perspectives in African Higher Education." In *African Higher Education: An International Reference Handbook*, 3–14. Bloomington: Indiana University Press.

UN Millennium Project (UNMP) (2005). *Toward University Primary Education: Investments, Incentives, and Institutions*. Task Force on Education and Gender Equality. London: Earthscan.

UNESCO (1995). *World Education Report 1995*. Paris: UNESCO Publishing.

UNESCO (1998). *World Education Report 1998*. Paris: UNESCO Publishing.

UNESCO Institute for Statistics (2001). *Sub-Saharan Africa Regional Report*. Paris: UNESCO. Download at http://www.eldis.org/static/DOC3023.htm

UNESCO (2002). *EFA Global Monitoring Report 2002. Education for All: Is the World On Track?* Paris: UNESCO. Download at http://portal.unesco.org/education/en/ev.php-URL_ID = 13603&URL_DO = DO_TOPIC&URL_S ECTION = 201.html

UNESCO (2003). *EFA Global Monitoring Report 2003/4. Gender and Education for All: The Leap to Equality. Sub-Saharan Africa Regional Overview*. Paris: UNESCO. Download at http://portal.unesco.org/education/en/ev.php-URL_ID = 25730&URL_DO = DO_TOPIC&URL_S ECTION = 201.html

UNESCO (2004). *EFA Global Monitoring Report 2005. Education for All: The Quality Imperative*. Sub-Saharan Africa Regional Overview. Paris: UNESCO. Download at http://portal.unesco.org/education/en/ev.php-URL_ID = 36071&URL_DO = DO_TOPIC&URL_S ECTION = 201.html

UNESCO (2005). *EFA Global Monitoring Report 2005. The Quality Imperative: Summary*. Paris: UNESCO. Download at http://portal.unesco.org/education/en/ev.php-URL_ID = 35874&URL_DO = DO_TOPIC&URL_SECTION = 201.html

UNESCO Institute for Statistics (2005). *Global Education Digest 2005. Comparing Education Statistics Across the World*. Download at http://www.uis.unesco.org/template/pdf/ged/2005/ged2005_en.pdf

UNICEF (2005). *State of the World's Children 2005*. New York: UNICEF.

Vavrus, Frances (2003). *Desire and Decline: Schooling Amid Crisis in Tanzania*. New York: Peter Lang.

World Bank (1989). *Sub-Saharan Africa: From Crisis to Sustainable Growth*. Washington, D.C.: The World Bank.

Index

Numbers in **bold italic** refer to captions.

Picture Credits

Contributors

PROFESSOR ROBERT I. ROTBERG currently holds the Fulbright Research Chair in Political Development at the Balsillie School of International Affairs in Waterloo, Canada. Prior to this, from 1999 to 2010 he served as director of the Program on Intrastate Conflict and Conflict Resolution at the Kennedy School, Harvard University. He is the author of a number of books and articles on Africa, including *Transformative Political Leadership: Making a Difference in the Developing World* (2012) and *"Worst of the Worst": Dealing with Repressive and Rogue Nations* (2007). Professor Rotberg is president emeritus of the World Peace Foundation.

DR. VICTOR OJAKOROTU is head of the Department of Politics and International Relations at North-West University in Mafikeng, South Africa. He earned his Ph.D. from the University of the Witwatersrand, Johannesburg, in 2007, and has published numerous articles on African politics and environmental issues. North-West University is one of the largest institutions of higher education in South Africa, with 64,000 students enrolled at three campuses.

SUZANNE GRANT LEWIS is the coordinator for the Partnership for Higher Education in Africa, a collaboration of seven U.S. foundations that supports the transformation of higher education in nine African countries. She earned her Ph.D. from Stanford University and has been awarded Fulbright fellowships for research (Tanzania) and teaching (South Africa). Dr. Grant Lewis was a faculty member at Harvard University's Graduate School of Education from 1997 to 2005, where she helped develop and direct Harvard's International Education Policy program. Her research focuses on policy efforts to address educational inequalities, including gender inequalities, in developing countries in democratic transition. She has worked with several universities in Namibia, Malawi, and South Africa. She also served as resident advisor to the Namibian and Malawian ministries of education (1992–1997).